BELLAMY

A Comedy-Farce in Three Acts

By Anthony Armstrong
and Arnold Ridley

Copyright © 1960 by Anthony Armstrong & Arnold Ridley
All Rights Reserved

BELLAMY is fully protected under the copyright laws of the British Commonwealth, including Canada, the United States of America, and all other countries of the Copyright Union. All rights, including professional and amateur stage productions, recitation, lecturing, public reading, motion picture, radio broadcasting, television, online/digital production, and the rights of translation into foreign languages are strictly reserved.

ISBN 978-0-573-01038-5

concordtheatricals.co.uk
concordtheatricals.com

FOR AMATEUR PRODUCTION ENQUIRIES

UNITED KINGDOM AND WORLD
EXCLUDING NORTH AMERICA
licensing@concordtheatricals.co.uk
020-7054-7298

Each title is subject to availability from Concord Theatricals,
depending upon country of performance.

CAUTION: Professional and amateur producers are hereby warned that *BELLAMY* is subject to a licensing fee. The purchase, renting, lending or use of this book does not constitute a licence to perform this title(s), which licence must be obtained from the appropriate agent prior to any performance. Performance of this title(s) without a licence is a violation of copyright law and may subject the producer and/or presenter of such performances to penalties. Both amateurs and professionals considering a production are strongly advised to apply to the appropriate agent before starting rehearsals, advertising, or booking a theatre. A licensing fee must be paid whether the title is presented for charity or gain and whether or not admission is charged.

This work is published by Samuel French, an imprint of Concord Theatricals Ltd.

The Professional Rights in this play are controlled by Eric Glass Ltd, 25 Ladbroke Cresent, London W11 1PS.

No one shall make any changes in this title for the purpose of production. No part of this book may be reproduced, stored in a retrieval system, scanned, uploaded, or transmitted in any form, by any means, now known or yet to be invented, including mechanical, electronic, digital, photocopying, recording, videotaping, or otherwise, without the prior written permission of the publisher. No one shall share this title, or part of this title, to any social media or file hosting websites.

The moral right of Anthony Armstrong & Arnold Ridley to be identified as authors of this work has been asserted in accordance with Section 77 of the Copyright, Designs and Patents Act 1988.

USE OF COPYRIGHTED MUSIC

A licence issued by Concord Theatricals to perform this play does not include permission to use the incidental music specified in this publication. In the United Kingdom: Where the place of performance is already licensed by the PERFORMING RIGHT SOCIETY (PRS) a return of the music used must be made to them. If the place of performance is not so licensed then application should be made to PRS for Music (www.prsformusic.com). A separate and additional licence from PHONOGRAPHIC PERFORMANCE LTD (www.ppluk.com) may be needed whenever commercial recordings are used. Outside the United Kingdom: Please contact the appropriate music licensing authority in your territory for the rights to any incidental music.

USE OF COPYRIGHTED THIRD-PARTY MATERIALS

Licensees are solely responsible for obtaining formal written permission from copyright owners to use copyrighted third-party materials (e.g., artworks, logos) in the performance of this play and are strongly cautioned to do so. If no such permission is obtained by the licensee, then the licensee must use only original materials that the licensee owns and controls. Licensees are solely responsible and liable for clearances of all third-party copyrighted materials, and shall indemnify the copyright owners of the play(s) and their licensing agent, Concord Theatricals Ltd., against any costs, expenses, losses and liabilities arising from the use of such copyrighted third-party materials by licensees.

IMPORTANT BILLING AND CREDIT REQUIREMENTS

If you have obtained performance rights to this title, please refer to your licensing agreement for important billing and credit requirements.

CHARACTERS

(in the order of their appearance)

PRITCHETT
LADY CAROLINE WAREHAM
SIR GEORGE WAREHAM
PAMELA WAREHAM
HECTOR C. ROBSON
BELLAMY
RICHARD WAREHAM
MAVIS MONTROSE
MORTIMER SEATON

SYNOPSIS OF SCENES

The action of the Play takes place in the lounge of "Barwell Towers", Sir George Wareham's house, near Tunbridge Wells, during the course of a week-end

ACT I
Friday evening

ACT II
Saturday morning

ACT III
Sunday morning

Time—the present

BELLAMY

ACT I

SCENE—*The lounge of Sir George Wareham's home, "Barwell Towers" situated near Tunbridge Wells.*

The room is typical of the lounge usually found in a large country house and bears ample evidence of being well lived in. Down R there is a big open fireplace and above it the wall slopes up towards the C at an angle of forty-five degrees. In this wall at RC are french windows which give on to a terrace and balustrade beyond which is the garden and distant woods. The garden is presumed to be reached by steps at the up C end of the terrace and on the terrace are garden chairs. Up C of the room is an alcove against the R and L walls of which are bookcases; in the L bookcase is a copy of "Who's Who". The wall then slopes away down L and at LC are double doors leading to the hall. Down L is a small door leading to another part of the house. The walls of the room consist partly of panelling and partly of bookcases; on the walls are a number of family portraits, sporting trophies and native weapons. In the wall R of the double doors is a bell. The furniture is heavy and comfortable, the most noticeable pieces being a large settee RC facing towards the fireplace and R of this is an armchair. There is an oak table LC with chairs above and R of it; on the table are magazines, a silver cigarette box, containing cigarettes, and a table lighter. There is a heavy desk L of the double doors on which is the telephone; there is a desk chair before it. Outside the double doors is a small table and another small table stands R of the double doors. A drinks cabinet stands up C in the alcove.

When the CURTAIN *rises it is about 3.30 p.m. on a sunny afternoon in late September and the french windows are open. The room is empty and the telephone rings loudly. For a moment it continues to ring and then* PRITCHETT *enters quickly* LC. *Pritchett is partly housekeeper and partly parlourmaid, an alert businesswoman of about fifty, dressed in a dark uniform with an apron.*

PRITCHETT. Barwell Towers . . . Yes, I think Lady Wareham is in. Who shall I say is speaking? . . . Oh, I'm so sorry, Mr Richard, I didn't recognize your voice. On the telephone everybody talks like everybody else . . . Yes, I'm quite well, Mr Richard, thank you . . . Oh, *sir*, I'm not all that old . . . (*Half laughing and half shocked*) What? . . . Of *course* I'm not making eyes at the new butler. You shouldn't *say* such things . . . Yes, I'll fetch your mother, Mr Richard —I think she's in the garden.

(PRITCHETT *puts the receiver on the desk and goes out through the french windows, and up* RC.

After a short pause, LADY WAREHAM *comes hurrying in through the double doors,* LC. *She is charming, about fifty, well dressed and very vague, one of those women who is always doing half a dozen things at the same time and achieving nothing at all. She is obviously in a great hurry, goes to the windows, stops, returns, crosses to the fireplace, stops again, goes once more to the windows and looks out to* L *and* R)

LADY WAREHAM. George dear, where are you? *George?* (*Without waiting for a reply, she comes back and crosses towards the door, down* L. *As she does so, she sees the phone receiver lying on the desk. She picks it up*) Tut, tut, tut! Why *won't* people put things back where they find them?

(LADY WAREHAM *replaces the receiver on the instrument and hurries out, down* L.
Just as she does so, SIR GEORGE WAREHAM *comes in,* LC. *He is about sixty, dressed in well-cut tweeds, a pipe in one hand and a paper under his arm*)

SIR GEORGE (*moving* C) Hello! Caroline! That you calling? (*He stands, looking round the room, and is about to go out again*)

(PRITCHETT *re-enters* RC)

Hello! That *you* calling, Pritchett?
PRITCHETT. No, Sir George. I was looking for her ladyship. There's a telephone call for her. It's Mr Richard.
SIR GEORGE. Dick, eh? Oh, all right, Pritchett. I'll take it. (*He crosses to the desk, pauses, and points to the instrument*) You've put the receiver back.
PRITCHETT. Oh, no, sir. I put it down by the side.
SIR GEORGE. Couldn't have done. Thing doesn't jump back the moment you leave the room—like a dog on an armchair. (*He picks up the receiver and shouts*) That you, Dick? . . . Dick! (*To Pritchett*) Not a sound of him. (*Holding out the receiver towards her*) Now what do I do?
PRITCHETT. Try dialling one-double-o, sir. The operator may get him back if he hasn't been cut off at his end yet.
SIR GEORGE. Right. (*He obeys the instruction*) Hello! Hello! You, the Operator? Has my son been cut off at his end yet? . . . What are you laughing for? Perfectly ordinary question. I want to speak to my son, who's just rung up, and now . . . Yes, I *know* the receiver was replaced, but *I* didn't replace it, so . . . Then how *do* I get him? . . . You mean if I wait he may come through again? Good! Fine! Good-bye, good-bye! (*He makes as if to replace the receiver on the instrument, changes his mind, lays it on the desk and turns with a triumphant look to Pritchett and points at it*) See?
PRITCHETT. Excuse me, Sir George.
SIR GEORGE. What's up?
PRITCHETT. If you leave the receiver off, Mr Richard won't be able to get you.

SIR GEORGE. 'Course he will. It was because the receiver was put back—by *someone*—he couldn't get me before, wasn't it? This time I'm all ready.

PRITCHETT. But he'll get "Number engaged", sir.

SIR GEORGE. Nonsense! How can it be engaged when I'm here waiting for him?

PRITCHETT (*explaining as tactfully as she can*) What I mean is *this*, sir. As far as *he'll* know the receiver will be off because you're speaking to someone else.

SIR GEORGE. But I *shan't* be . . . (*Staring owlishly at her until the penny drops*) D'you know—I believe you're right, Pritchett. (*He replaces the receiver on the instrument*)

(*As he does so,* LADY WAREHAM *comes hurrying in again, down* L. *She is carrying a bowl of withered dahlias*)

LADY WAREHAM. Oh, George, so *here* you are—I've been looking for you *everywhere*.

SIR GEORGE. But I've been in my study ever since lunch.

LADY WAREHAM. Oh, no, you haven't. I've just come down from your study and you weren't there.

SIR GEORGE. 'Course I wasn't. I'd just left. Went straight to the hall, and then I heard you calling, and came . . .

LADY WAREHAM (*interrupting and pointing to the desk*) George! Why *will* you leave the telephone receiver off?

SIR GEORGE. So it was *you* who put it back?

LADY WAREHAM. Of course I did. You know how pressed we are for money.

SIR GEORGE. What the deuce has that got to do with it?

LADY WAREHAM. I should have thought it was obvious. If you leave the electric light on it runs up the bills, doesn't it? So if you leave the receiver off . . .

SIR GEORGE. I did *not* leave the receiver off. It was Dick!

LADY WAREHAM. Really, George, what a ridiculous excuse. Dick hasn't been here for a month.

SIR GEORGE. He was *on the line*! He wanted to speak to you.

LADY WAREHAM. Richard on the line! Why couldn't you have said so in the first place? (*She gives him the flowers and hurries to the desk*)

(SIR GEORGE *stares stupidly at the flowers*)

PRITCHETT (*as Lady Wareham is about to lift the receiver*) Excuse me, m'lady, Mr Richard is not on the line now.

LADY WAREHAM. Then how on earth can he speak to me? Really, you're all being very unhelpful.

PRITCHETT. He *was* on the line, m'lady, and then you put— (*correcting herself*) then he was cut off. He is expected to ring again any minute.

LADY WAREHAM (*to Sir George*) If only you hadn't left the receiver off none of this bother would have occurred.

(SIR GEORGE *starts to expostulate*)

And *why* are you holding that absurd bowl of flowers? Give them to Pritchett.

PRITCHETT (*taking them*) What shall I do with them, m'lady?

LADY WAREHAM (*at a loss*) Well—I—oh, give them to Bellamy. He's sure to know why I had them. Oh, of course! I saw them in the study and they were dead. They're to be thrown away.

(*The telephone rings*)

Ah! (*She lifts the receiver*)

(PRITCHETT *goes out* LC)

Yes, *of course* this is Barwell Towers . . . Lady Wareham speaking. Hello! Hello! Yes! Oh, is that *you*, Richard? . . . Yes, that's right . . . It was your father's fault. He did something stupid to the telephone and put it out of order. Where *are* you, Richard? . . . (*To Sir George*) He says he's in a call-box near Edenbridge. (*Into the receiver*) What on earth are you doing there? . . . Yes, *I know* you're coming down for the week-end, but . . . (*Becoming very serious*) Mavis? . . . Tch! Tch! It's *extremely* inconvenient. (*To Sir George, disgustedly*) He's bringing that girl!

SIR GEORGE. *What* girl?

LADY WAREHAM. You know—*that* one. We met her in London. Mavis—what was it?—Montrose. (*Into the receiver again*) Eh? . . . No, I was talking to your father . . . But, my dear Richard, I would have sent her a proper invitation—that is, if we'd wanted her to come, but . . . And there's another thing, too. Mortimer is arriving tomorrow . . . What? . . . *Please,* don't refer to Mortimer Seaton as Pamela's "boy friend"—it's vulgar . . . No, you can't talk to Pamela: she's gone for a walk . . . What? . . . No, of course I can't *refuse* to have her, if you're already half-way here. But it's *most* awkward . . . All right, Richard . . . Soon after tea. Yes . . . Good-bye. (*She replaces the receiver and turns to Sir George*) It's *most* inconsiderate of him. Anyone would think we were running a hotel.

SIR GEORGE (*darkly*) Not *yet.*

LADY WAREHAM. What do you mean?

SIR GEORGE. Well, lots of people in our position are doing some damn funny things to raise money these days. Got to. And so shall *we*, it looks to me. That infernal mortgage, fixed rents and all the rest of it. And the interest you get from things like War Loan is ridiculous. However! This Mavis wench—we've got a room for her, haven't we?

LADY WAREHAM. That's not the point. I don't think the girl is *suitable*.

SIR GEORGE (*with an earthy chuckle*) That depends what one wants her to be suitable *for*. (*He sits above the table* C)

LADY WAREHAM. George! You know what I mean.

SIR GEORGE. 'Pon my soul I don't. She seemed all right to me.

LADY WAREHAM. You're always so *wrong* about people, George. Why when you first met *Mortimer*, you didn't like him.

SIR GEORGE. Naturally not. Fella didn't hunt.

LADY WAREHAM. He's good looking, perfect manners, and *very* well off. Pamela seems to think the world of him and they're practically engaged. That's the main thing.

SIR GEORGE. The main thing to *me* is that the chap's obviously rolling in the stuff.

LADY WAREHAM. He'll certainly be able to give Pamela a happy life.

SIR GEORGE. Yes. And me, too.

LADY WAREHAM. What on earth do you mean?

SIR GEORGE. With all that Stock Exchange knowledge of his and what not, I'm hoping to pick up some useful tips about raising cash.

LADY WAREHAM. George! Don't be mercenary!

SIR GEORGE. All very well to say that, but with costs going up, dividends coming down, workers coming out and roofs coming off . . .

LADY WAREHAM (*alarmed*) *What* roofs?

SIR GEORGE. Didn't you know? Those blasted cottages down by Ricks Beyond. Norgate was up about it this morning.

LADY WAREHAM. Anyway, roofs have nothing to do with this Mavis. The next thing we shall hear is that Richard wants to marry her.

SIR GEORGE. Nonsense. A fella doesn't marry every girl he asks away for a week-end. Dammit, *I* didn't. (*He chuckles reminiscently*)

LADY WAREHAM. I *beg* your pardon.

SIR GEORGE (*hastily*) Nothing, nothing. (*He clears his throat*) Forget it. There's nothing wrong with the girl—that is, to look at. Damn good legs.

LADY WAREHAM. I wish you'd concentrate more on her upbringing and less on her physical attractions.

SIR GEORGE. Not half so interesting. Anyway, what's wrong with her upbringing? I know she's an actress, but fellas have married actresses before, haven't they? Lord Pressleigh, for instance.

LADY WAREHAM. Madge Pressleigh wasn't an actress—she was in the chorus. *Quite* different.

SIR GEORGE. Don't tell me you're so old-fashioned you hold it against a girl because she's an actress?

LADY WAREHAM. Of course not. But she's not quite—quite out of the top drawer. And if he does marry her and they have a boy, he'll inherit the baronetcy. We must face facts.

SIR GEORGE. Don't see what we can do about it, though. If we bar the girl the house . . .

LADY WAREHAM. He'll put her up at an hotel somewhere and then there's no knowing *what* would happen.

SIR GEORGE. Could have a jolly good *guess*. (*Again he chuckles*)

LADY WAREHAM. Kindly refrain from being coarse, George.

SIR GEORGE. Dammit all! One moment you tell me to face facts and the next not to be coarse. Facts *are* coarse—leastways, most of 'em that come *my* way. (*He looks at his watch and gets up*) Blast! Asked Norgate to come up and talk about those infernal roofs at half past three. Cost two-fifty at least, and God knows where that's coming from. (*He starts off towards the double doors*)

LADY WAREHAM. George! Wait!

SIR GEORGE (*turning*) What's up now?

LADY WAREHAM. Those flowers. What have you done with them? I'm sure when I came in I had a bowl of flowers. I was going to do something with them.

SIR GEORGE. Oh, those! You told Pritchett to give them to Bellamy.

LADY WAREHAM. Don't be absurd. Why should I send flowers to the butler?

SIR GEORGE. Dead. That's why.

LADY WAREHAM (*in a panic*) George! *Don't* tell me Bellamy's *dead!* He mustn't be—not with guests arriving.

SIR GEORGE. Well, he wasn't dead ten minutes ago. Saw him in the hall. Walking quite briskly, too.

LADY WAREHAM. Then why did you say he *was?* I do wish you'd try to *concentrate*.

SIR GEORGE. I will. On those damn roofs.

(SIR GEORGE *goes off* LC. LADY WAREHAM *looks after him in her usual state of bewilderment. She crosses quickly to the fireplace, decides she has no idea why and crosses again in the direction of the door, down* L.

As she reaches it, two figures appear RC *on the terrace from up* C *and enter. One is* HECTOR C. ROBSON, *a good-looking American of about thirty-two. He wears a rather highly coloured sweater with a polo collar, well cut fawn slacks and smart white and tan shoes. But he is by no means a caricature, being pleasantly unassuming and well mannered. His voice is quiet and his accent of the Southern States. With his arm around her waist, he is supporting* PAMELA WAREHAM. PAMELA *is nice, typically English, and aged about twenty-seven. She wears a short-sleeved lightly coloured blouse, a tweed skirt and sensible walking shoes. A slightly bloodstained handkerchief is bound around her left arm*)

PAMELA. Here we are at last!

LADY WAREHAM (*turning in the doorway*) My dear Pamela! *Really!*

PAMELA (*with Hector's arm still around her*) Hello, Mother! (*She realizes the reason for Lady Wareham's surprise and disengages herself*) Oh—perhaps I'd better explain.

LADY WAREHAM (*grimly*) I think you *had!*

PAMELA. It's quite simple, really. I'll introduce you. This is Mr —(*turning to Hector*) I'm terribly sorry but I'm afraid I don't know your name.

HECTOR. Robson. (*Bowing politely*) Hector C. Robson.

PAMELA. Mr Robson, Mother. (*To Hector*) My mother—Lady Wareham.

HECTOR (*bowing again*) I hope you find yourself well, ma'am.

LADY WAREHAM. At the moment I find myself somewhat *surprised*.

PAMELA (*lightly*) Don't be silly, darling.

LADY WAREHAM. I'm *not* being silly. When I see my daughter with a young man's arm around her and learn that she does not even know his name . . .

PAMELA. We've only just met. Mr Robson is an American.
LADY WAREHAM. That may make his behaviour understandable but not altogether *acceptable*. Will you please tell me *how* you met?
PAMELA. Certainly, Mother. He's just shot me.
LADY WAREHAM. *Shot* you? Really, Pamela! This is no time for foolish jokes.
PAMELA. It *isn't* a joke, but it's not serious.
LADY WAREHAM. It must be one or the other.
PAMELA. Actually, it's perfectly simple. I was walking through Larch Bottom...
HECTOR. And I was shooting rats down by that old stack at the roadside when a big fat fellow ran out and off into the underbush. I let fly with my gun...
PAMELA. And one of the pellets just nicked my arm. (*Showing her bandage*) Look!
LADY WAREHAM (*in sudden panic*) Then it's *not* a joke—it's *true?* He *did* shoot you! (*Rushing to the phone*) I'll get Dr Rawlings at once. (*Snatching off the receiver*) What's his number?
PAMELA (*stopping her*) Mother! Please! It's absolutely *nothing!* The merest scratch. (*Crossing to the settee and sitting*)

(LADY WAREHAM *replaces the receiver*)

But it was a bit of a shock at the time, and Mr Robson very kindly said he'd bring me home.
HECTOR. It seemed the least I could do.
PAMELA. Now you understand how we met.
LADY WAREHAM. Do I? It seems rather a peculiar method of introduction. (*She adds*) Even for an American.
HECTOR (*hastily*) Matter of fact, ma'am, I've seen you before. Down in the village—one day last week. You were coming out of a store with a mound of parcels. You kept dropping them off and I kept picking them up.
LADY WAREHAM (*acidly*) How kind! But I don't remember your face.
HECTOR. Maybe it was behind all the parcels.

(PAMELA *laughs*)

LADY WAREHAM (*frowning at her and changing the subject*) And have you been in England long, Mr—er——
HECTOR (*smiling*) —Robson. No, only about a month this trip. I've rented a tiny place called *Elm Tree Cottage* way down beyond Larch Bottom, but I aim to stay over quite a while.
LADY WAREHAM. Why?
HECTOR. Well, you see, it's this way: I'm writing a book.
PAMELA. *Are* you? How exciting! What's it about?
HECTOR. England.
LADY WAREHAM. Impossible!
HECTOR (*smiling and unruffled*) *Difficult*, but not...
LADY WAREHAM. How can you write a book about a country when you've only been in it a month?

HECTOR. Fact is, I've been over here before. I was stationed in Lincolnshire in the U.S. Air Force for quite a while. Then—after I'd gone home to the States I had an urge to come back again. You see, ma'am—I *love* this country.

LADY WAREHAM (*mollified*) *Everyone* does, you know.

PAMELA. Except practically every *other* country in the world!

HECTOR. You can take it from me that England's swell, ma'am, swell!

(LADY WAREHAM *winces*)

(*Noticing*) Or should I be calling you "your ladyship" or something?

LADY WAREHAM. "Lady Wareham" is customary. Not that I'm the least concerned *how* you address me, Mr Robson.

HECTOR (*missing the snub completely*) Now that's mighty civil of you, Lady Wareham. But—as a matter of fact—I was asking out of curiosity. You see, I'm aiming in my book to explain all your peculiar habits and customs to the folks our side, and one of the things they can never dope out is your English title racket.

LADY WAREHAM (*cuttingly*) How very interesting! Pamela, if you won't see a doctor, I insist on your having some disinfectant and a bandage. I'll get the first-aid box. (*Crossing to Hector*) So we won't detain you any longer, Mr Robson! I'm sure you want to get back to your book.

HECTOR. There's no hurry—no hurry at all. I've written all I want for today.

LADY WAREHAM. Your *shooting* then.

HECTOR (*grinning at Pamela*) And I guess I've *shot* all I want for today, too!

LADY WAREHAM. But—well—(*realizing she is defeated*)—if you insist on staying . . .

HECTOR. That's very kind of you, Lady Wareham. I will—but only for a short while, I'm afraid.

LADY WAREHAM. Then—well . . . !

(*Words fail her.* LADY WAREHAM *goes to the door down* L, *turns to glare at* HECTOR, *who has risen and now smiles and bows. She makes a last effort to think of something crushing, shrugs her shoulders and goes out*)

HECTOR. Say, Miss Wareham . . . (*Breaking off*) Here, pardon me. I suppose you've got a title, too?

PAMELA. No. I'm just plain "miss".

HECTOR. But surely—if your father's a lord . . . ?

PAMELA. He's not. Just "Sir George".

HECTOR. That *lower* than a lord?

PAMELA. Lower than *all* lords.

(HECTOR *looks surprised*)

You see, there are several kinds—barons, viscounts, earls.

HECTOR. Well, what d'you know? (*Bringing out a little notebook*) This is tougher than I guessed. D'you mind . . . (*He puts the book away*)

Oh, say! Pardon! Y'know, Miss Wareham, this is the very first time I've ever met any of the British aristocracy in—well—in their own reservation—if you'll pardon the expression—and it's impressed me no end. Your mother's manner to me, for instance, the way . . .

PAMELA (*apologizing*) I know, but you see—she was a bit startled . . .

HECTOR. That calm way of setting a guy at his ease . . .

PAMELA. What!

HECTOR. So different from way back in the States where first thing you know people rush at you and slap you on the back and thrust a Scotch into your hand and . . .

PAMELA (*faintly*) I can hardly imagine mother doing that!

HECTOR. Exactly! See what I mean?

PAMELA. But talking of that, I *could* do with a drink. I suddenly feel a little . . . Well, you see, I've never been under fire before. There may be some brandy in that cupboard. (*She rises*)

HECTOR (*intervening*) No. You stay right there. I'll get it.

PAMELA. I expect you can do with one yourself. It must have been a shock to you, too.

HECTOR. It sure *was*, Miss Wareham. When I found . . . (*Overcome*) Say, what *would* have happened if I'd hurt you seriously?

PAMELA (*lightly*) Probably the village would have lynched you. They're all a bit het-up about two recent burglaries we've had in the neighbourhood.

HECTOR. Guess I'd have deserved it at that.

PAMELA. But, as you *didn't*, I shouldn't worry. There are glasses there, too. (*She indicates the cupboard and lies back on the settee*)

HECTOR. O.K. (*He goes* C *to the cupboard, opens it and looks inside*) You certainly know how to make a guy welcome over here. (*He begins searching the cupboard*)

(SIR GEORGE *enters* LC. *Pamela, on the settee, is hidden from him, but he sees Hector. He stands staring for an instant, and then rushes forward and grabs him by the neck*)

SIR GEORGE. *Got* yer! (*He drags Hector to his feet*) Caught you red-handed!

(HECTOR *struggles*)

Oh, no, you don't. You're not getting away with it *this* time!

HECTOR. Here, I say! (*Struggling*) Hell! Leggo!

SIR GEORGE. Not on your life!

PAMELA (*jumping up from the settee*) Father! Have you gone *mad?*

SIR GEORGE. *Got* the fella! At *last!*

(HECTOR *breaks from him*)

Shut the windows, Pamela! Don't let him make a bolt for it! (*He dances about like a rugger full-back, arms extended, between the two doors on the* L *of the room*)

HECTOR. Here! What's the idea? (*He goes to Pamela for protection*)

SIR GEORGE (*very excited*) Get away from her! Don't let him come near you, Pamela! (*He tries to snatch a terrifying weapon, say, a yataghan, from the wall*) Damn this blasted wire! (*He struggles to free the weapon*)

(LADY WAREHAM *comes in down* L. *She is carrying a first-aid box*)

LADY WAREHAM. George! What *are* you doing?

SIR GEORGE (*frantically*) Shut that door, Caroline! Ring the police! Call Bellamy! *Do* something, woman! Don't stand looking like a goldfish! Hurry!

LADY WAREHAM. I don't understand, George!

SIR GEORGE. Dammit got eyes, haven't you? I've caught that blasted burglar, of course! Got him red-handed! Ring the *police*, I tell you!

PAMELA. No, Mother! Don't! It's all a mistake, Father!

SIR GEORGE. What d'you mean—mistake? (*Pointing at Hector*) Who is this fellah? (*Turning to Lady Wareham*) D'*you* know, Caroline?

LADY WAREHAM. Well, yes.

SIR GEORGE (*calming down*) Oh! Oh, I see.

LADY WAREHAM. He's just shot Pamela, dear.

SIR GEORGE. *What!* (*He rushes at Hector again*)

(HECTOR *breaks away towards the window*)

PAMELA (*grabbing hold of Sir George and restraining him*) *Accidentally*, Father. That's why he's here. I met with an accident and he brought me home.

SIR GEORGE. And then starts rifling the room . . .

PAMELA. No! He was getting the brandy. I *asked* him!

SIR GEORGE (*glaring at Hector*) Then if you're not the burglar, why the blazes didn't you say so?

HECTOR (*still feeling his neck*) Well . . . You see . . .

PAMELA. You didn't give him much opportunity, Father.

SIR GEORGE. Oh! (*After a pause, calming down*) Hum! Ha! Seems to have been a bit of a mix-up. Looks as if I owe you an apology, Mr—er . . .

PAMELA. Robson. Mr Robson's an American, Father.

SIR GEORGE. *American*, eh? Oh, I see. So that's why he shot you. Always shooting each other over there, I understand. (*To Hector, with interest*) You one of those gangster fellahs one hears about, eh? Been wanting to meet one. (*He advances to shake hands*)

PAMELA. Father!

LADY WAREHAM. There now! I didn't introduce you properly. (*Formally to Hector*) This is my husband—Sir George Wareham. Though, of course, you've already met.

HECTOR (*rubbing his neck*) Already met! Well, I've heard *some* British understatements but . . .

SIR GEORGE (*shaking hands again*) How d'you do?

HECTOR. Glad to meet you, Sir George Wareham, or do I call you "Sir Wareham"?

SIR GEORGE. Sir Wareham! Well, hardly. "George" is more usual.

HECTOR. Now isn't that really friendly of you, George.

SIR GEORGE (*double-taking*) Eh?
HECTOR. I mean, at such short acquaintance, too.
LADY WAREHAM (*who has been looking vaguely at the first-aid box*) Now—what have I brought this for? (*Remembering*) Oh, yes—Pamela! Your arm.
PAMELA. Oh, leave it, Mother—please! (*Pulling down the handkerchief*) See! It's not even bleeding now. It barely broke the skin.
LADY WAREHAM (*looking helplessly at the box*) Then what shall I do with this?

(HECTOR *rubs his neck*)

(*She sees and advances upon him*) Perhaps *you'd* like . . .
HECTOR (*retreating hastily*) No, no, thanks, Lady Wareham. I'm fine! I sure am. Never even broke the neck—I mean the skin.
LADY WAREHAM. That's all right then. (*For no reason at all she hands him the first-aid box*)
HECTOR (*obliged to take it; trying to explain to Sir George*) I'm terribly sorry about the accident. You see I wasn't expecting a girl to be in the woods. I was just out shooting girls—I mean rats—and . . .
SIR GEORGE (*laughing*) Shooting girls! Hey! That's good! (*Immensely taken with it, and pointing an imaginary gun at the ceiling*) Girl over! Bang-bang! Got her! *My* girl, I think, Lord Tyson! (*He positively roars with laughter*)
LADY WAREHAM (*interrupting icily*) George! (*He stops laughing abruptly*) Don't be puerile.
PAMELA. Father, do you know Mr Robson is writing a book. About us. He's come over to study us.
SIR GEORGE. Good God! What's he think we are—apes?
HECTOR. No, not exactly . . .
SIR GEORGE (*rounding on him*) What d'you mean—"not *exactly*"? That's insulting. Not content with shooting my daughter you say we're . . .
HECTOR (*embarrassed*) Oh, I didn't mean that. I meant the book's not exactly about *you three* but *all* English people.

(SIR GEORGE *grunts non-committally*)

I mean—well, you're a grand nation, but lots of Americans—my father, for instance, is one of them—are—well, a bit anti-British.
SIR GEORGE (*incredulous*) You mean he doesn't *like* us?
LADY WAREHAM (*drifting aimlessly about, obviously looking for something*) How disgraceful!
HECTOR. Oh, nothing *personal*, believe me, Lady Wareham. Just a sort of—general attitude.
LADY WAREHAM (*face to face with him*) Ah! *There* it is! (*Taking the first-aid box away from him*) Now—what was I—oh, yes! Pamela dear, your arm.
PAMELA. But, Mother darling—I've *told* you. (*Resigned*) All right! (*She takes the first-aid box*) I'll go upstairs and bathe it, if it'll make you happy. (*Crossing towards Hector*) I won't say good-bye because I'm sure we shall meet again.

HECTOR. I certainly hope so, Miss Wareham. After all, I'm not far away.

PAMELA (*sweetly*) No—almost within gunshot, one might say. 'Bye!

(PAMELA *exits* LC)

HECTOR (*as she goes*) Good-bye. (*To Lady Wareham*) Guess I'd better be hitting the trail, too.

LADY WAREHAM (*looking around nervously*) Oh, no—please don't do that!

SIR GEORGE. No, wait a bit, wait a bit! Don't go yet, Robson. (*He places Hector in the armchair*)

(LADY WAREHAM *is annoyed*)

Now—tell me. I can't get over what you said—your father not liking the British. (*He sits on the* R *end of the settee, leaning forward with his hands on his knees*) I mean—why not?

HECTOR (*embarrassed*) Well—you know how it is. My pop—he's —he's a man of the people . . .

LADY WAREHAM (*coldly*) Oh, I *see!*

SIR GEORGE. Don't interrupt, Caroline—this is important. (*To Hector*) Go on.

HECTOR (*still embarrassed*) Put it this way. Pop's not had much upbringing and has never been out of the States, barely even out of his home town—Florence, in South Carolina—and that's not a big burgh either. So he's got kinda fixed in his ideas, and one of them is that the British are all high-hat.

SIR GEORGE. Rubbish. Rarely worn these days. Only weddings, Ascot and so forth.

HECTOR (*struggling further*) I mean ritzy, toney, aristocratic. Sort of different from . . .

LADY WAREHAM (*cutting in coldly*) Different from a man of the people, or as we should say, of the working classes. (*She sits on the downstage end of the settee*)

HECTOR. Well, if you care to put it like that . . .

(LADY WAREHAM *sniffs and looks very superior, but* SIR GEORGE *displays a kindly interest*)

SIR GEORGE. Working man, hey? Nothing to be ashamed of in that. We can't all be millionaires. What's his trade?

HECTOR. I guess you could call it building.

SIR GEORGE. Well, that's good solid employment. No reason for him to have such ridiculous ideas as not liking the British.

HECTOR. Say, don't get me wrong, please! Pop's attitude cuts no ice with me at all. I love the British, and he would, too, if he'd gotten to understand them like I have. But the trouble with him is that all his ideas of what the English are like have come from wayback pulp magazines, old-time stage Britishers, typical Englishmen in our early films—dukes with monocles, galloping about the country shooting foxes and what not.

(SIR GEORGE *shudders, aghast at this blasphemy*)

And he doesn't like it because they *aren't*.

LADY WAREHAM. And what is his idea of us that we aren't?

HECTOR. Well, I've been over here quite a bit and *I* know you're all grand people who mix-in almost the same as Americans. Real democratic. I saw over a castle once and there was an old guy in filthy clothes on his knees planting things in the garden. I spoke to him and—what d'you know—it seemed he was the boss—Lord whatzit himself! But according to pop—he should have been sitting on a dais in a coronet and robes, with flunkeys buzzing around serving him champagne.

LADY WAREHAM. Absolutely ridiculous!

HECTOR (*getting up; triumphantly*) I know, I know! For instance, look at you two here! Sir George and Lady Wareham, behaving just plain ordinary, fetching bandages and jumping on burglars, instead of calling half a dozen footmen and so forth. Now my pop would expect you to be wearing—well, not robes and coronets perhaps, but decent aristocratic clothes instead of filthy . . . (*He breaks off, looking first at Sir George's well-cut tweeds and Lady Wareham's nice frock, and lets that one go*) Well, pop would expect you to be sitting around doing nothing, but just waiting for a dignified butler to bring afternoon tea on a silver tray. But *I* know that you don't act that way and that you're just . . . (*He turns while walking and breaks off suddenly*)

(*The double doors have opened and* BELLAMY *appears carrying a silver tea tray set for tea, followed by* PRITCHETT *with a cake-stand.* BELLAMY *is, in manner, the perfect butler to end all butlers. He is, however, not the pompous, stout, elderly type, such as P. G. Woodhouses' "Beach", but more like "Jeeves"; he is not more than forty, posing as thirty-seven or thirty-eight. He is not the young self-possessed butler of today—a cross between a valet and a footman—for dignity, solidity and reliability are his keynotes. He wears discreet side-whiskers*)

Well, I'll be . . . (*He looks at Sir George and Lady Wareham, but both are completely unmoved, and adds hastily*) Guess I've said enough about pop and his ideas!

SIR GEORGE. Ah! Tea! Good!

(*In complete silence, every movement followed in awed amazement by* HECTOR, BELLAMY *places the tray on the small table* L *and moves it nearer to* LADY WAREHAM, *who starts to adjust the cups and generally fuss about.* BELLAMY *takes the cake-stand from* PRITCHETT *and gives her a curt nod of dismissal.*

PRITCHETT *goes out, after which he places the cake-stand at Sir George's elbow and is about to make a dignified exit*)

LADY WAREHAM (*looking at the tray*) We shall require another cup for Mr Robson, Bellamy.

BELLAMY (*bowing slightly*) Very good, m'lady.

HECTOR (*coming to life but still staring at Bellamy*) Not for me, thanks, Lady Wareham. I gotta go.

SIR GEORGE. What's that? Must have a cup of tea first.

(BELLAMY *is waiting and regarding space with a completely expressionless stare*)

HECTOR. No, thanks, I . . . (*With a look at Bellamy*) I just can't take any more. (*He moves* R.)

LADY WAREHAM. Oh, you've had tea already?

HECTOR (*dithering a little, the shock not yet over*) No, I . . . Well, yes . . . Mind if I go out this way? (*He moves to the windows* RC) I left my gun by that little gate.

LADY WAREHAM. By all means. Good-bye!

HECTOR. I'll be seeing you again perhaps. And Miss Wareham, too.

SIR GEORGE (*rising*) Ha! Yes! (*He repeats his imaginary gun business*) Girl over! Bang-bang! Got her! *My* girl, Lord Tyson! (*He laughs heartily until he is stopped by a look from Lady Wareham*) Hrm! Good-bye then—for the present.

HECTOR (*escaping hastily*) Good-bye, good-bye, Lady Wareham. (*With a last look at Bellamy*) Well—what d'you *know?*

(*Mopping his brow*, HECTOR *disappears up* C *along the terrace*)

LADY WAREHAM (*starting to pour out*) What an extraordinary young man! Still, I don't suppose you can expect much from a working-class background.

SIR GEORGE. Oh, I don't know. He's quite passable considering.

(BELLAMY, *who has remained in the background, gives a discreet cough*)

LADY WAREHAM. What is it, Bellamy?

BELLAMY. I am given to understand by Pritchett, m'lady, that Mr Richard is expected this evening . . .

LADY WAREHAM. Oh, yes. And he's bringing a friend with him—a Miss Montrose.

BELLAMY. Yes, m'lady. The oak room is, I believe, reserved for Mr Mortimer Seaton, who arrives tomorrow. Would you wish me to put her in the turret room or the blue room?

SIR GEORGE. The blue room.

LADY WAREHAM (*firmly*) The turret room.

BELLAMY (*addressing Sir George*) Very good, Sir George—the turret room. (*He moves solemnly to the double doors, opens them, turns, holding a door in each hand and facing his employers*) I will instruct Pritchett to place suitable flowers in the young lady's chamber.

(*With a dignified bow*, BELLAMY *takes a couple of paces backwards and closes the double doors behind him*)

SIR GEORGE. Flowers in her . . . What a perfectly *extraordinary* idea!

LADY WAREHAM (*sharply*) George!

SIR GEORGE. Oh, I see. Still, wherever he puts 'em he made it sound as if the girl was going to lie in state or something. (*He takes a cup of tea from Lady Wareham*) Poor old Morrison never spoke like that.

LADY WAREHAM. Maybe not. But with *all* his qualities, Morrison was not quite so good a butler.

SIR GEORGE. One knew where one was with him though. This fellow's a bit funny at times.

LADY WAREHAM. What *do* you mean? He's as sane as I am.

SIR GEORGE. Well, that's not a good . . . (*He thinks better of it*) I don't mean he's half-batty. But—well, that way he has of never going out of a room without stopping in the door to make some sort of—pronouncement. Just now, f'rinstance. Morrison used to (*with a gesture*) just go *out*. With this fella you somehow have to *watch* him go.

LADY WAREHAM. That doesn't make him a worse butler. He's a treasure. In fact, he's—what's the word I want? Something to do with hens?

SIR GEORGE. Hens! You mean broody?

LADY WAREHAM (*testily*) No, no. Oh—of course—impeccable.

SIR GEORGE. What we see of him, yes. But I was in the gun-room one day soon after he arrived and overheard Pritchett telling him —quite nicely—something about cleaning the silver, and other things a butler *should* have known—and I got the impression he didn't. (*He offers her the cake-stand*)

LADY WAREHAM. You probably misunderstood. Don't forget all those excellent families he was with.

SIR GEORGE. Ah, yes. Wonderful references I must admit. All three peers of the realm, too. Who was the chap—Lord Whatwasit —who said that being forced to part with such a splendid retainer was the unhappiest moment of his whole life?

LADY WAREHAM. Yes, and another one wrote that Bellamy could always be relied upon in any situation—even if it were outside the scope of his duties.

SIR GEORGE. Hm! That's a bit what I mean. I'd prefer a chap who had a proper grasp of his duties *inside* his scope—such as cleaning silver—before he started being relied on *outside* it.

LADY WAREHAM. But if he hadn't been an excellent all-round butler, surely one of his previous employers would have hinted as much to you when you took up his references whatever he'd written? People are so non-committal on paper.

SIR GEORGE (*chuckling*) Think so? You should read some of the breach-of-promise cases . . . But here! Why should anyone hint to me?

LADY WAREHAM. Because you took the references up.

SIR GEORGE. No, no. *You* took them up.

(PAMELA *enters* LC)

PAMELA. Ah! Tea! Good! (*She comes and sits in the armchair and starts to eat a sandwich*)

(LADY WAREHAM *pours a cup of tea*)

LADY WAREHAM (*pouring tea*) I'm quite certain, George, *I* didn't take them up.
PAMELA. Take what up?
LADY WAREHAM. Bellamy's references, dear. Your father did it, but he seems to think that I . . .
SIR GEORGE (*interrupting*) Think? I *know*. I distinctly remember giving all three letters to you because you said you'd do it.
LADY WAREHAM. And I distinctly remember handing them back because—because . . . Well, I must have had *some* good reason.
PAMELA (*affectionately*) You are the maddest pair of darlings.
LADY WAREHAM (*triumphantly*) And you put them in your wallet.
SIR GEORGE. No.
LADY WAREHAM. You did.
SIR GEORGE (*triumphantly taking out his wallet*) Quite impossible. Because if I had, they'd be there now, wouldn't they? (*Opening his wallet*) And you can see for yourself that . . . (*He finds the three letters*) —er—they do happen to be . . .
PAMELA (*bursting into laughter*) Oh, *Father!*
LADY WAREHAM (*complacently*) There! That's all settled satisfactorily.
PAMELA. But is it? It means neither of you has done anything *about* the references.
SIR GEORGE (*rising*) Going to do something *now*, though. Ring up these fellahs right away. (*Tapping the letters*) One or more of them may give me the tip if there's really anything funny about Bellamy. (*He goes to the phone and starts looking at the letters and consulting the phone directories*)
PAMELA (*to Lady Wareham*) I don't understand. Why should there be anything funny about him?
LADY WAREHAM. Your father thinks he doesn't know a butler's duties properly—and won't just (*with a gesture*) go out.
PAMELA. How absurd! Bellamy's a poppet.

(*There is a reaction from* LADY WAREHAM)

Anyway, isn't it a bit late for checking references? Suppose one of these people says: "I wrote all those nice things because I'm softhearted: actually Bellamy swipes the port and tickles the housemaids." I mean, you couldn't suddenly get rid of him.
LADY WAREHAM. But I don't want to . . .

(BELLAMY *enters* LC)

BELLAMY (*addressing Lady Wareham*) I thought you might care to know, m'lady, that Mr Richard and his companion have arrived. They did not stop at the front door but drove straight round to the garage. No doubt they will come direct through the garden.
PAMELA (*finishing her tea and getting up*) I'll go and meet them.

(PAMELA *goes out* RC)

LADY WAREHAM. Thank you, Bellamy. See to their luggage, will you? And please tell Pritchett I'll ring for her later on to show Miss Montrose to her room.

BELLAMY. Very good, my lady.

(*As he is about to go,* SIR GEORGE, *looking rather baffled and without having telephoned, comes back to Lady Wareham with the letters in his hand.*

BELLAMY *recognizes them with a sudden uneasiness and goes out thoughtfully*)

SIR GEORGE. This is damned odd.

LADY WAREHAM. What is, dear?

SIR GEORGE (*holding up one letter*) From Lord Illingworth, Half Moon Street, W.1. But no telephone number on it, and not in the directory. (*He looks at the letter*) No house number, either. *Must* have one. Fella can't live all over the street. (*He looks at another letter*) And this Lord Aldingham. Just *Harwood House*, Suffolk. It's . . . (*He breaks off as cheerful voices are heard off*)

(PAMELA *enters* RC, *followed by* DICK *and* MAVIS. *Dick is about twenty-eight, ebullient, and knows his own mind. Mavis is about twenty-four, a pretty and obviously practical girl, normally self-possessed, though at the moment a little awed by surroundings to which she is not entirely accustomed, and nervous of being in Dick's home for the first time. She is practically a lady*)

DICK (*hurrying to Lady Wareham and hugging her*) Hullo there, Mum! How goes it? (*To Sir George*) And the old man? Still bearing up?

(*They reply suitably*)

(*He takes Mavis by the hand*) Mum, you've met Mavis, of course?

LADY WAREHAM. Oh, yes. In London.

MAVIS (*with eager nervousness and speaking a little too quickly*) Yes, that was it. Dick asked me to lunch, you remember, specially to meet you. At the *Savoy*, too. Really grand. Though, of course, for *you* it . . . (*She breaks off, more formally*) It's awfully nice of you to have me—especially at such short notice.

LADY WAREHAM. I'm afraid I had very little alt . . .

SIR GEORGE (*interrupting her quickly*) A great *pleasure*, m'dear. Did you have—er—a good run down?

DICK. Smashing. We ran down a hen.

LADY WAREHAM (*casually*) Did you really? Nobody we know, I trust.

PAMELA. Mother! He said a *hen!*

LADY WAREHAM (*sympathetic*) Oh, poor *thing!* I thought he just said a *man.* (*She goes* L *to the bell and rings it*)

DICK. Cost me a quid. (*To Sir George*) I say, I presume the character I glimpsed at the front door as we whizzed past was the new butler chap. Looked absolutely wonderful.

SIR GEORGE. Yes, that was him. (*Correcting himself*) He. No, dash it him. Oh, anyway it was.

LADY WAREHAM (*to Dick*) Have you had tea, Richard?

DICK. We had it on the road, Mum, thanks.

LADY WAREHAM (*to Mavis*) I expect you'd like to see your room and tidy up.

MAVIS (*hand to hair*) It *would* be nice. That open car of Dick's is like a wind tunnel test.

PAMELA. *I'll* take her.

LADY WAREHAM. It's all right, dear. I've already rung for Pritchett.

MAVIS. Yes, please don't bother.

(PRITCHETT *enters* LC)

DICK (*gaily*) Hullo there, Pritchett. Recognize me now I'm not wearing a telephone?

PRITCHETT (*overcome, but pleased*) Oh, Mr Richard! The things you say!

DICK. You're looking younger than ever.

PRITCHETT. Oh! Oh, dear!

LADY WAREHAM. Stop giggling, Pritchett. Miss Montrose would like to see her room.

PRITCHETT. Very good, m'lady. (*To Mavis*) This way, please, miss. (*She moves down* L)

DICK. We'll be here when you come down, Mavis. Then you can see the garden before it gets too chilly.

MAVIS. That would be lovely.

(MAVIS *smiles at them and follows* PRITCHETT *out down* L)

DICK (*after a pause*) Sorry I shot you sitting, Mum. About having Mavis here at such short notice.

LADY WAREHAM. Well, it was rather . . .

SIR GEORGE (*interrupting*) Talking of shooting. (*He starts to chuckle*) Funny thing, but we had a bit o' shooting here today. American fella who's staying at *Elm Tree Cottage*—he shot Pamela in Larch Bottom.

DICK (*laughing*) What? Sounds painful, Pam. (*Turning her round*) Let's see.

PAMELA (*laughing*) Don't be a fool, Dick.

DICK. Seriously, though, it's not true?

PAMELA (*nodding*) Only a graze on the arm. Nothing at all, really. But it's given father quite a lot of good clean fun.

SIR GEORGE (*delightedly*) Girl over! Bang-bang! Got her . . .

LADY WAREHAM. Not *again*, please, George. Go on with whatever you were doing about those references.

SIR GEORGE. But I wasn't doing *anything*. I can't trace the fellows. (*He looks at the letters again*) Lord Illingworth? Lord Porteous? Don't remember ever *hearing* of them. Ah, wait a minute! (*With an idea*) Who's Who! (*He puts the letters on the table and goes to the bookshelf up* L *during the following dialogue*)

DICK. What's the trouble?

LADY WAREHAM. Your father's making a great fuss about a simple thing like checking Bellamy's references.

DICK. Checking? But the chap's been here for . . .
PAMELA. The fact is, Dick, each of our dear parents thought the other had done it.
DICK. Lord, what a family! (*He picks up the letters and looks at them*)

(SIR GEORGE *comes back* c *with "Who's Who", opening it as he does so*)

SIR GEORGE. Now! Lord Illingworth? (*He turns a page or so*) Illingworth.
DICK (*reading the letters*) I say! These are pretty good, aren't they, Pam?
PAMELA (*looking over his shoulder*) They certainly are.
SIR GEORGE. Dashed funny thing! No Illingworth here! Who are the other two?
DICK (*briefly referring to the letters*) Lord Porteous and Lord Aldingham. (*He speaks absently, his mind evidently on something else as he compares the letters carefully*)

(SIR GEORGE *meanwhile is turning further pages*)

(*After a pause, suddenly*) I say!
LADY WAREHAM. What is it, dear?
DICK. Dunno quite. But it's just struck me that the handwriting in all these three letters is rather—well, *similar*.
PAMELA (*still looking*) Goodness! Yes, it is.
LADY WAREHAM. But what an extraordinary coincidence, when they're from three different people.
SIR GEORGE (*looking up from "Who's Who"*) Here! This beats everything! *None* of 'em are in here. It's most . . . Eh? What's that about handwriting?
DICK (*slowly*) Pam and I are just wondering whether these letters mightn't all have been written by the same person. (*He hands the letters to Sir George*)
LADY WAREHAM (*suddenly aghast*) Really, Richard! You're surely not suggesting that they're *forgeries?*

(SIR GEORGE *merely stares at the letters*)

PAMELA. You must admit that it's a possibility.
SIR GEORGE (*bursting out*) Written by the same . . . Fellas not in *Who's Who* . . . No proper addresses . . . (*Quite overcome*) Good Lord! (*He hands the letters to Dick and sits* R *of the table*)
PAMELA. What on earth do we do now?
LADY WAREHAM (*brightly*) Let's ask him if he wrote them himself.
DICK. *Dear* old mum!
LADY WAREHAM. And if he did, that's all right, because he's the person most concerned and ought to *know* if he's a good butler.
PAMELA (*gently*) That's a lovely idea, darling.
LADY WAREHAM (*beaming*) I thought you'd like it.
DICK. I think, Dad, you'd better start by sounding him out—

tactfully—about his previous employers, and see what he's got to say.

Sir George (*vaguely*) Sound him out?

Dick. Yes. Ask him if . . . Ssh! (*He breaks off, and all look enormously unconcerned*)

(Bellamy *enters* LC)

Bellamy. May I take the tea things out, my lady?

Lady Wareham (*flustered*) Eh? Oh, yes. Sound the tea things out, Bellamy . . . I mean, take . . . Yes, please do.

(Bellamy *advances and takes first the tea tray, which he carries out and puts on a table just outside the double doors. During this everyone in the room looks expectantly at Sir George and while Bellamy is momentarily outside with the tray,* Dick *and* Pamela *signal earnestly to Sir George*)

Sir George (*testily*) Got to think it out!

(Bellamy *returns for the cake-stand, and* Sir George *starts to hum, "pom-pompomming" extremely casually, till* Pamela *nudges him hard, indicating* Bellamy *now on his way out with the cake-stand*)

(*Stopping pom-pomming; indignantly*) All right. All right. (*He clears his throat loudly*) Oh! Ah! Bellamy!

Bellamy (*turning*) Yes, sir?

Sir George. You've—you've been with us a fortnight now, haven't you? D'you like it here?

Bellamy. Extremely, sir.

Sir George. Good! Good! (*At a loss*) Er—good!

Bellamy (*again with an uneasy glance at the letters in Dick's hand*) It was kind of you to enquire, sir. (*He turns again towards the double doors, with the cake-stand*)

Dick (*in a low, urgent voice*) Father! (*He thrusts the letters into Sir George's hand*)

Sir George. Eh? Oh, yes. (*Awkwardly*) Er—Bellamy!

Bellamy (*turning again*) Sir?

Sir George. About these—these three references?

Bellamy (*looking a little hunted*) Yes, sir?

Lady Wareham (*suddenly*) Did you write them yourself, Bellamy?

(*Everyone is aghast at this question*)

Pamela. Mother! (*Hastily*) That is—we mean . . .

Bellamy (*recovering after a brief start*) But, of course, m'lady.

(Pamela *and* Sir George *are taken aback.* Lady Wareham *is smiling and nodding happily*)

Sir George. B—but . . . But then, dammit . . .

Bellamy (*imperturbably*) I made those copies because I wished to keep the originals in my possession. It is the usual practice.

Lady Wareham (*sweetly, as though she had known all this*) There you are, you see.

Bellamy (*obviously anxious*) Is anything amiss, sir?

SIR GEORGE. No, no. Oh, dear me, no. Not at all, no . . .
PAMELA (*quickly*) All three of them seem to have thought very highly of you, Bellamy.
BELLAMY. I have always endeavoured to give satisfaction, miss.
SIR GEORGE. Yes, that's quite the . . .

(PAMELA *gives him a fierce look*)

(*He catches it*) All right! All right! Hrm! This Lord Porteous—don't think I know him—he treated you all right, I hope. (*He puts the letters on the corner of the table*)
BELLAMY. With great consideration, sir. Lord Aldingham, on the other hand, was extremely lively.
SIR GEORGE. And Lord—er . . .
BELLAMY. Lord Illingworth, sir. Ah, there was a *real* gentleman (*With meaning*) He always used to say he had the most complete trust in me.
SIR GEORGE. Quite, quite! (*With extreme casualness*) As a matter of fact I—er—chanced to be glancing through *Who's Who*, and I just didn't happen to see their names down there.
BELLAMY (*obviously taken aback, but recovering*) Lord Porteous, sir —if I recollect—had quarrelled with the editor and would not permit an entry. And—let me see—Lord Illingworth was particularly averse to what he called vulgar publicity.
SIR GEORGE. And the other johnnie . . .?
BELLAMY. Lord Aldingham, sir?

(SIR GEORGE *nods*)

Well, he . . . (*With an idea*) May I be permitted to inspect the volume? (*He puts down the cake-stand and approaches the table*)
SIR GEORGE. Certainly. (*He hands the book over*)
BELLAMY (*studying it*) Ah, as I thought, sir. A nineteen-thirty-eight *Who's Who*.
SIR GEORGE. Haven't been able to afford one since.
BELLAMY. That would explain it, sir. (*With finality*) Lord Aldingham was hardly "Who" at that time. (*He puts the volume down on the corner of the table on top of the letters, at the same time skilfully abstracting the latter from underneath, and without being noticed he holds them concealed behind his back*) Will you be requiring anything further, sir?
SIR GEORGE. No. Don't think so.
BELLAMY. Very good, sir. (*He turns round to pick up the cake-stand and unobtrusively slides the letters into his coat pocket. He then moves with the cake-stand to the double doors, where he turns and speaks, startling Sir George*)

(SIR GEORGE *turns back to the others*)

If I may venture the remark, sir, in all sincerity, I find my present situation far more rewarding than my previous ones.

(BELLAMY *goes out* LC)

DICK (*after a pause*) Well, Dad, he seems to have explained everything. If you believe him.

SIR GEORGE. Not so sure. It's dashed mysterious. Peers are *always* in *Who's Who*—even when they're still only What. And as for vulgar publicity . . . Something fishy somewhere.

LADY WAREHAM. I wish you wouldn't use that word, George. It makes me think of the way breakfast kippers hang on in the dining-room.

SIR GEORGE (*getting heated*) I will if I like. Fishy. Fishy. Fishy.

(LADY WAREHAM *puts her handkerchief to her nose*)

I refuse to leave things as they are. If the people who gave him those references don't exist, it's more than fishy, it's . . .

LADY WAREHAM. Supernatural?

SIR GEORGE. Exactly. (*Suddenly shouting*) No!

DICK. Here, hold hard! We've got to be certain before we start anything. (*He picks up "Who's Who"*) You're the only person, Dad, who's looked these people up, and you know how muddle-headed . . . (*Hastily*) I mean, you may not have looked in quite the right place. (*Opening the book*) I'll just check up. Now what were their names again? (*He sits above the table*)

SIR GEORGE (*feeling in his pockets*) Let's see. Where are those references.

PAMELA. Lord Porteous was one.

(MAVIS *comes in down* L, *having tidied up and maybe changed her frock*)

DICK (*turning the pages*) Lord Porteous. Porteous?

MAVIS (*surprised*) Who on earth's talking about Lord Porteous?

SIR GEORGE. We are. Dick's looking him up . . . (*He stops searching his pockets*) Hey! Do *you* know the fella?

MAVIS. Well, in a way. (*She puts her bag on the armchair*) You see, he's a fairly well-known character . . .

SIR GEORGE. Well, I'm blest! Here we are wondering if he even exists, and you *know* him.

DICK (*putting down the "Who's Who"*) Do you really, Mavis?

MAVIS (*nodding, puzzled*) But what is it all about?

PAMELA. Our new butler gave us a reference from him. He's one of his previous employers.

MAVIS (*surprised*) What?

SIR GEORGE. Or so he says.

DICK. Yes, we've just realized that that reference, *and* two others, didn't have proper addresses and, in fact, couldn't be checked.

MAVIS (*evidently understanding something which they don't*) Oh, I *see*. And who were the other—employers?

SIR GEORGE. A Lord—Lord Illingworth.

(MAVIS *nods, smiling, as if she had guessed*)

And—let's see—Lord Elderham, wasn't it?

MAVIS. Don't you mean Aldingham?

PAMELA. That's right. But do you know him, too?
MAVIS (*gravely*) Again, in a way. In fact, all three of them.
DICK (*getting up*) Then that's all right. If these people are real, Dad, and Mavis knows them, then everything's O.K. Don't let's bother further. (*He crosses* R) Come on, people! The garden!

(DICK *goes out* RC *to the terrace. The others start drifting* R. MAVIS, *however, not picking up her bag*)

MAVIS (*as she reaches the windows*) And you find your new butler quite satisfactory?
LADY WAREHAM. Excellent.
SIR GEORGE. Except that he never goes out of a room without stopping to make a remark in the doorway. Gets on my nerves.

(MAVIS *starts to laugh*)

What's funny about that, young woman?
MAVIS (*apologizing*) Nothing, Sir George! Just a sudden thought. I'm so sorry. Butlers (*with a slight emphasis on the word*) don't usually do that, do they?
SIR GEORGE. This one does.

(DICK *has already gone into the garden.*
MAVIS *goes out to the terrace, followed by* LADY WAREHAM *and* SIR GEORGE)

(*Off; on the terrace*) Well, come along and see our dahlias. We've a dashed good show this year.

(MAVIS *moves on out of sight*)

LADY WAREHAM (*following*) Yes. But I still maintain that Reverend Morton oughtn't to be in the same bed as Chorus Girl.
SIR GEORGE (*following*) Nonsense! They show each other off beautifully.

(*The room is now empty.*
After a pause, BELLAMY *enters* LC. *He sees "Who's Who", picks it up, looks at it, rubs his chin reflectively, and then takes it back to the bookshelf and hides it behind other books. He returns and starts to tidy up illustrated papers on the table*)

MAVIS (*off*) No, no, you go on, Dick. I know just where I left it. I'll catch you up.

(MAVIS *enters* RC *and now picks up her bag from the chair. Seeing Bellamy, she starts a polite "Good evening", but breaks off in the middle with a little exclamation, staring incredulously at him, hand to mouth*)

Trevor!
BELLAMY (*equally incredulously at the mutual recognition, and speaking in his own voice, not as the butler*) Mavis! I never for a moment thought. But you're Mavis Fenton. They said a Miss *Montrose*.
MAVIS (*absently, still staring at him*) I was offered a small part in a West End show. Fenton didn't sound very—very West End, so I

changed ... (*Breaking off*) Trevor, what on earth are you doing here? (*Indicating his clothes*) And like that?

BELLAMY (*a little sharply*) Come to that, what are *you* doing here? (*He gestures to the french windows*) Like that?

MAVIS (*defiantly*) Looking after myself.

BELLAMY (*bitterly*) Bettering yourself?

MAVIS. If you put it that way, yes. (*She pauses then goes to him*) Trevor, I could be very happy, I know. Are you going to give me away?

(BELLAMY *is silent, obviously considering*)

Are you going to spoil things?

BELLAMY (*after consideration*) I don't see that I *can* very well, because (*indicating his clothes*) I don't want *you* to give *me* away.

MAVIS. You've given yourself away already.

BELLAMY (*very upset*) Oh, no.

MAVIS. Only to me—so far.

BELLAMY. Then it looks like a bargain between us.

MAVIS. Yes. (*With a thought*) Unless ... Trevor, *why* are you doing this? Have—have you any sort of—of game on?

DICK (*calling off before Bellamy can answer*) Mavis! Come along. (*Approaching*) What's keeping you?

(BELLAMY *goes quickly to* LC *as* MAVIS *turns* RC)

MAVIS (*calling*) Coming, darling. (*She turns back at the window*)

(BELLAMY *turns at the doors*)

BELLAMY (*the butler once more*) Whether or no I have a—hem—game on, miss, is a question the answer to which must be deferred to a later occasion.

CURTAIN

ACT II

SCENE—*The same.*

When the CURTAIN *rises it is about 9.30 the next morning and the sun is shining brilliantly through the french windows and on to the terrace outside.* PRITCHETT *is tidying some things on the mantelshelf, and* SIR GEORGE *is speaking on the telephone. Whatever may be the discussion, the person on the other end is doing most of the talking, and it is obvious that* SIR GEORGE *is hearing a most disturbing piece of news.* PRITCHETT *continually reacts to some of his most explosive comments.*

SIR GEORGE (*on the phone*) Yes, yes, yes, but how? . . . No, did he? . . . The scoundrel! . . . This is beyond a joke . . . Good Lord! . . . Something will have to be done, no doubt about it, Buster old man . . . I'll come right over . . . No, no, you must have someone reliable to discuss it with. It's a blasted . . . Yes, right away—*now* . . . Good-bye, Buster.

(SIR GEORGE *puts down the receiver and hurries out through the french windows in a storm of excitement. After a pause,* PRITCHETT *finishes her job and moves towards the double doors.*

MAVIS *enters down* L)

PRITCHETT. Oh, good morning, miss. It's a *lovely* morning, too, isn't it? Breakfast is in the dining-room.

MAVIS (*smiling*) Yes, I know. I've had mine. (*Awkwardly*) Er—could I—I mean . . . (*She hesitates*)

PRITCHETT. Yes, miss?

MAVIS. I—I wonder if I might speak to the butler?

PRITCHETT. Yes, miss. (*She makes a move to go and then turns*) Is it anything *I* could help in, miss?

MAVIS. No, it's just something I wanted to tell him.

PRITCHETT. Certainly, miss. I'll ask him to come at once.

(PRITCHETT *goes out* LC. MAVIS *looks round the room and then takes a cigarette from the silver box on the table and lights up.*

BELLAMY *comes in by the double doors*)

BELLAMY (*gravely*) You wished to see me, miss? (*He looks round the room, then speaks in his own voice; urgently*) Look here, Mavis, I just can't make it out. You said last evening you'd guessed about me before you'd even *seen* me. How on earth had I given myself away.

MAVIS (*smiling*) When I hear that a so-called butler can never leave the room without giving himself an exit line, *and* I hear that he has had false references from a Lord Porteous and a Lord Illingworth and a Lord Aldingham . . .

BELLAMY (*with a faint smile*) They weren't exactly false. I *have* been butler to them all, and others too, as you well know.

MAVIS. I do. Remember, I've been maid to similar—employers. But only on the *stage*. Because they aren't real people, but characters in plays. And the butler isn't a real butler, just an actor.

BELLAMY. I am a real butler now.

MAVIS (*warmly*) You'll never be real. You'll go on living in a stage world, thinking stage, breathing stage, eating stage, relating every damn thing that happens around you to stage, stage, stage.

BELLAMY (*equally warm*) And why not? Doesn't life run almost exactly on stage lines? Every single damn thing that happens around me is a stage situation. (*Bitterly*) Even you turning up here out of the blue when I thought I was safe.

MAVIS (*laughing suddenly*) You're safe enough with me, Trevor. And I'm enjoying watching you. You were absolutely *marvellous* at dinner last night. Didn't you see me in the front row of the dress circle? I just couldn't take my eyes off you.

BELLAMY (*complacently*) One *can* rather *hog* the show with no author or producer to hamper one.

(MAVIS *offers him a cigarette from the silver box*)

(*He is about to take it but stops*) No. Butlers are only supposed to take those on the sly.

MAVIS (*laughing and putting the box down*) When the management isn't in front, eh? (*Suddenly serious*) Trevor, I haven't had a chance to see you alone till now. And in a few minutes I've got to go out picking mushrooms with Dick. Tell me—why *are* you doing this?

BELLAMY. Can't you guess? You *should*, you know.

MAVIS. You're not suggesting it has anything to do with *me*, are you?

BELLAMY. Didn't you once tell me—at Huddersfield, I think it was—that I was a ham actor, only fit for the small butler parts I played?

MAVIS. Did I? Yes, I think I *did*. I suddenly got mad at you for not asserting yourself more. And I still get furious when I think of Jimmy Waite, without an "h" to his name, playing the duke— and you the same old butler.

BELLAMY (*sadly*) It was really the only part I *could* play—at least, it was the only sort of part they ever *gave* me. But you rubbed it in a bit, didn't you?—saying that *being* a butler was about all I was fit for.

MAVIS. I was angry. I didn't really mean it.

BELLAMY. Then you *should* have done—it was true! (*Stopping her from interrupting*) No, no, don't *apologize*, my dear—I'm very grateful to you. This is much better than being an *actor*—regular pay, all found, a position of authority, no moving into lousy fresh digs every week. *And* no train journeys.

MAVIS (*nodding her head in sad remembrance*) *Oh*, those changes at Crewe on wet Sundays.

BELLAMY. With the pubs just shut . . .

MAVIS. And not reopening till after . . .

BELLAMY. You'd left for Rochdale! Remember?

MAVIS. I certainly *do!* (*With a sudden change*) Seriously, though—I must speak to you.

BELLAMY. About young Dick?

(MAVIS *nods*)

I suppose you want to tell me you're in love with him?

MAVIS. I *am* in love with him.

BELLAMY. Sure?

MAVIS (*ignoring this*) And he's in love with *me*. We're going to be very happy.

BELLAMY (*gravely*) I see. Just as a matter of interest—have you told him you've been married before?

MAVIS. Of course. Right at the start I told him I'd had a short and unhappy marriage and that my husband had left me.

BELLAMY. Letting him infer you were divorced, I suppose?

MAVIS (*defiantly*) Well, why not? I'd been faithfully *promised* a divorce, hadn't I—the very moment I asked for it? So it wasn't of real significance.

BELLAMY. All the same, I think he ought to be told. You see . . .

MAVIS (*interrupting him angrily*) Oh, yes, I know! You want to build up some damn stage scene, don't you? You're already picturing me taking Dick by the hand and saying in a low earnest voice: "Promise you won't be angry, darling, but there's something I must tell you." Then a lovely "come-clean-at-last" confession. Well, there's nothing doing! This is *life*, not the stage—and things don't happen that way.

BELLAMY. Oh, yes, they do. I see it here every day.

MAVIS. Not with *me* you won't! And don't you dare tell him yourself!

BELLAMY. I can't very well, can I? Didn't we agree last night not to give each other away? Besides, I particularly want to stay in this job.

MAVIS. Yes. There is *that*, I suppose. (*With a new thought; slowly*) You know I can't really believe that you've become a butler here just for the reasons you've given.

BELLAMY. Can't you? They seem pretty sound ones to me.

MAVIS. There *must* be something else—some——

BELLAMY. —some game, eh? That's what you asked me last night, wasn't it? Well—the answer is—no game at all.

(DICK *comes in by the double doors in sports coat and flannel trousers and carrying a basket. Hearing someone enter, but without turning,* BELLAMY *resumes his butler role*)

Would there be anything further, miss?

DICK (*from just inside the door, before she can answer*) All ready, Mavis?

MAVIS. Just coming, darling. (*She gives Bellamy a meaning look as she passes him on the way to the door*)

(BELLAMY *bows gravely*)

DICK (*as they go out*) Brook Meadow's the best place. It's not far, and there was a heavy dew last night.

(DICK *and* MAVIS *go out through the double doors.*
Left alone, BELLAMY *goes out on to the terrace is seen unfolding and and arranging garden chairs, passing out of sight down* R *as he does so.*
After a short pause LADY WAREHAM *comes hurrying in* LC. *She carries a breakfast cup and saucer*)

LADY WAREHAM. George, I've brought... (*She sees that the room is empty*) George, where are you? Really, you're *too* tiresome! Pamela! Where are *you?* (*She crosses to the door down* L *and calls*) Pamela! George! (*Louder*) *George!*

(BELLAMY *appears in the french windows and gives a little cough.*
LADY WAREHAM, *hearing it, speaks as she turns*)

Ah, there you are, darling!

(BELLAMY *reacts, startled*)

I've been looking everywhere for you.

BELLAMY (*politely*) *Have* you, m'lady?
LADY WAREHAM. No, not you, dar... I mean Bellamy. It's Sir George I'm looking for.
BELLAMY (*gravely*) Inevitably, m'lady.
LADY WAREHAM. I wanted something, only I can't remember what. (*She absently hands him the coffee-cup*)
BELLAMY (*looking at it*) Perhaps it was to have your coffee-cup refilled?
LADY WAREHAM. Of course not. That's Sir George's cup. He didn't finish it when he was there, so I brought it out because he was here and now he isn't and can't.
BELLAMY (*all at sea*) I—I quite understand, m'lady. (*He begins to move away with the cup*)
LADY WAREHAM. One moment, Bellamy.

(BELLAMY *turns back*)

Where is Sir George?
BELLAMY. I am informed he was *here* some while back—telephoning, m'lady.
LADY WAREHAM. I *know*. That's why he left the breakfast table. He jumped up suddenly and said: "Good Heavens! I've forgotten to ring old Buster!"
BELLAMY (*surprised*) Buster, m'lady?
LADY WAREHAM. Colonel Maltravers, of course. He's always called "Buster".
BELLAMY. Not by *me*, m'lady.
LADY WAREHAM (*ignoring this*) He dashed out of the room. And now—(*with a gesture*) he's disappeared.
BELLAMY. No doubt, m'lady, he will (*repeating the same gesture*) reappear.
LADY WAREHAM (*doubtfully*) I wonder. Something funny is going on.

BELLAMY. You mean, inexplicable occurrences are afoot, m'lady?
LADY WAREHAM. What on earth are you talking about? I mean that after ten minutes I sent Miss Pamela to look for him, and now *she's* vanished, too!
BELLAMY. I believe Miss Pamela is with the American gentleman who called yesterday.
LADY WAREHAM. Robson?
BELLAMY. Exactly, m'lady. A few minutes ago I observed him coming up the drive. And then I saw Miss Pamela go out to meet him.
LADY WAREHAM. Impossible! You're certain of that?
BELLAMY (*having his own little joke*) That, m'lady, is definitely what the butler saw.
LADY WAREHAM (*suddenly*) Had he a gun?
BELLAMY. A gun? I think *not*, m'lady.
LADY WAREHAM (*relieved*) Thank heaven for that. It would be inexcusable if he shot her again. All the same it's extremely tiresome and ... (*Suddenly*) Why on earth are you holding that cup, Bellamy?
BELLAMY (*lapsing into his normal voice, before he can stop himself*) Because you gave me the damn ... (*Quickly recovering*) I understand you desired it should be removed, m'lady.
LADY WAREHAM. Well, *remove* it, and then search for Sir George. (*Adds*) He must be *somewhere*, mustn't he?
BELLAMY. I should envisage that as a distinct possibility, m'lady. (*He moves to the double doors and turns to deliver his usual exit line*) May I say, m'lady ... (*He breaks off, much annoyed*)

(MORTIMER SEATON *appears on the terrace outside the window.* MORTIMER *is clean-shaven with dark brushed-back hair and very good-looking—perhaps excessively so—about thirty-five, easy of carriage and address, with perfect manners. In fact, a slightly "sleek" type of young man. He always seems at ease, and possesses a charm which, after a while, one rather suspects of being "turned on" to create a good impression. He wears a beautifully cut suit and carries two expensive-looking cases. A light overcoat is thrown over one shoulder*)

LADY WAREHAM (*turning and seeing him*) Why, Mortimer! (*She rushes towards him*) How *nice* to see you!
MORTIMER (*easily*) Charming of you to say so, Lady Wareham. Actually, I was afraid I was terribly early and ...

(*As* LADY WAREHAM *seems determined to shake hands with him,* MORTIMER *is compelled to put down one of his suitcases. But the instant he does so,* LADY WAREHAM *picks it up and staggers with it towards Bellamy, leaving* MORTIMER *with an outstretched hand*)

LADY WAREHAM. Take Mr Seaton's luggage, Bellamy.
BELLAMY (*aggrieved into lapsing into his own voice again*) But I was going to ... (*Recovering himself*) Certainly, m'lady.

(*As* BELLAMY *passes* LADY WAREHAM, *she takes the cup from him and he collects Mortimer's other bag, hat and overcoat*)

Allow *me*, sir. (*He starts towards the double doors*)
LADY WAREHAM. You're in the turret room, Mortimer.
MORTIMER (*smiling his best*) The turret room—that's grand.
BELLAMY (*turning and coughing discreetly*) Excuse me, m'lady. I think you will find that Miss Fent—er—Miss Montrose is in the turret room.
LADY WAREHAM. Don't be absurd, Bellamy. Miss Montrose is out gathering mushrooms with Mr Richard.
BELLAMY (*very patiently*) Exactly, m'lady. What I meant was that Miss Montrose is *sleeping* in the turret room.
LADY WAREHAM. But I was certain she . . . You don't mean *she's gone back to bed?*
BELLAMY (*after taking a deep breath and raising his eyes to heaven*) I mean that Miss Montrose has been allocated the turret room and Mr Seaton—so I was given to understand—is to occupy the oak room.
LADY WAREHAM. Then *don't* take his luggage to the turret room.
BELLAMY (*again aggrieved into using his own voice*) But I wasn't going to . . . (*Recovering*) Certainly not, m'lady. (*He moves to the double doors and turns*) 'Twould indeed be a comedy of Eros.

(BELLAMY *makes a dignified exit with the luggage*)

LADY WAREHAM (*turning to Mortimer*) What *does* he mean? And why *will* he always have the last word? It worries George quite a lot. (*Standing by Mortimer, she gives him the coffee-cup*)

(MORTIMER *absently takes it*)

That reminds me—George has disappeared.
MORTIMER (*worried*) Disappeared? No? Since when?
LADY WAREHAM. Nearly half an hour ago.
MORTIMER. Oh, I see. That's not very alarming, is it?
LADY WAREHAM. You never know with George . . . He once completely disappeared for under ten minutes. I was hoping you'd seen him.
MORTIMER. I'm afraid not. You see, I got a lift in a friend's car and he's only just dropped me at the little gate. I say, I hope you don't mind my turning up like this when you were expecting me on the twelve-fifty. But this friend was motoring down to Hastings early this morning and . . . (*Finding the coffee-cup in his hand, he automatically raises it to his lips*)
LADY WAREHAM (*stopping him*) Excuse me—I think that's *George's* coffee.
MORTIMER (*staring incredulously at the cup—not at all certain how he came by it*) I say! I'm sorry!
LADY WAREHAM (*taking it from him*) Not at all. What *will* Bellamy do next?
MORTIMER (*recovering quickly*) Actually—if you're sure it's convenient, I'm quite glad to get here early. There's a little business matter I want to discuss with Sir George.

LADY WAREHAM (*placing the cup on the desk by the telephone*) Oh, don't do that. (*Turning*) Please!
MORTIMER (*taken aback a little*) But—it was at *his* suggestion.
LADY WAREHAM. I know, I know! That's what worries me. George is absolutely helpless when it comes to business. *Whatever* he advises you to do, I *beg* of you not to do it.
MORTIMER. Well—I rather thought *I* was to advise *him*.
LADY WAREHAM. Oh, that's *quite* different. Absolutely splendid—if you can find him, of course. Oh, by the way, Pamela's disappeared, too.
MORTIMER (*disturbed*) Pamela—*disappeared*.
LADY WAREHAM. Yes. She's gone off with an American. It was what the butler saw.
MORTIMER (*upset*) You mean—she isn't coming back?
LADY WAREHAM. I most sincerely hope she is—and as soon as possible—the house is full of people, turning up at such *unexpected* hours, too—so much to arrange.
MORTIMER (*relieved*) Oh, I see. You don't mean she's run away from home, then?
LADY WAREHAM. Run away? What an absurd suggestion! Of course not! (*Archly*) Not with *you* coming for the week-end.
MORTIMER. Thank you.
LADY WAREHAM (*going to him suddenly and shaking hands*) I'm so glad you've arrived safely and there's not the slightest need to apologize for being late—the trains are *terrible* these days.

(MORTIMER *starts to correct her*)

Now perhaps you'll excuse me. I've something important to do, and as long as I stay here chatting I shan't remember what it is. (*She goes to the double doors*) You might like to take a walk in the garden. (*She turns at the double doors, smiles, seems about to say something but stops*) Dear me, I'm getting like Bellamy.

(LADY WAREHAM *goes out. Left alone*, MORTIMER *stares after her for a few seconds, shakes his head and gazes round the room. After a pause, he takes some papers out of his pocket, obviously connected with his "business" with Sir George, and glances through them in a self-satisfied way. He replaces them in his pocket, strolls to the window, where he suddenly sees someone and calls*)

MORTIMER. Pam! Hello! Pam!
PAM (*off*) Why, Mortimer!

(PAMELA *comes hurrying in through the windows*)

We didn't expect you so early.
MORTIMER. I got a lift, darling. (*He takes her in his arms and kisses her*)

(PAMELA *manages to disengage herself quickly although not obviously*)

PAMELA. Lucky man!
MORTIMER. I *am* indeed.

PAMELA. I meant—getting a lift.

MORTIMER. Aren't you glad?

PAMELA (*without particular enthusiasm*) Why—of course. (*She quickly turns back to the french window and calls*) Where have you got to, Mr Robson?

(HECTOR *enters*)

I didn't mean to desert you like that, but our guest has arrived. Let me introduce you—Mr Robson—Mr Mortimer Seaton.

MORTIMER (*coolly*) How d'you do?

HECTOR. Glad to know you, Mr Seaton. (*He insists on shaking hands*)

PAMELA. Mr Robson is an American, Mortimer.

MORTIMER (*irritated by Hector's arrival and allowing his charm to lapse for once*) So I gathered.

HECTOR (*seeing no offence as usual*) Yup, I give it away pretty quick, don't I?

PAMELA (*quickly*) And how's the great business world, Mortimer? All the bulls and bears eating out of your hand, I hope? (*To Hector*) Mr Seaton is—how exactly *do* you describe yourself, Mortimer—something in the City?

HECTOR (*before Mortimer can reply*) Big business, eh? Now that's mighty interesting. What's your firm, Mr Seaton?

MORTIMER. Well—I'm my *own* firm—in a way.

HECTOR. Free of all the combines, eh? Well, perhaps . . . (*He breaks off, looking at him suddenly*) Say! Haven't we met some place before?

MORTIMER. Most unlikely, I should say.

HECTOR (*thoughtfully*) Maybe, but . . . You been over in the States?

MORTIMER (*after hasty consideration*) Well—yes—but only twice. Very short visits, too.

HECTOR (*stroking his chin*) Y'know, I'm fairly good at remembering faces . . .

MORTIMER. So am I. That's why I'm sure you're mistaken. (*Changing the subject*) By the way, are you—are you week-ending here, too?

HECTOR. Oh, no, I *live* here.

MORTIMER (*not liking this*) Oh?

PAMELA. Mr Robson has taken a cottage near Larch Bottom.

HECTOR. And I only met Miss Wareham yesterday—a most unfortunate accident.

PAMELA (*mocking*) Sir, you say the sweetest things!

HECTOR (*confused and contrite*) Oh, I didn't mean it *that* way! (*To Mortimer*) I meant I was out shoot . . .

PAMELA. Now! Now! I told you, as we came up, not to mention that.

MORTIMER (*resenting the suggestion of a secret between them*) I don't follow. Won't someone tell me?

PAMELA. It's nothing, really. Only everyone's trying to keep quiet about it because father won't. He's seized upon it as a heavy joke. (*She glances at Hector*)

(HECTOR *briefly raises an imaginary gun and laughs*)

And it's driving mother and me crackers. Dinner last night was the end.
MORTIMER. Oh, I see, darling.

(*The word "darling" registers on* HECTOR, *who looks quickly from one to the other*)

I know your father when he gets a joke between his teeth. (*To Hector*) Are you over here for long?
HECTOR. Well, I guess it kind of depends.
MORTIMER (*coldly*) Oh, I see.
PAMELA (*to Mortimer*) Mr Robson's writing a book—about English customs.
MORTIMER. What? Oh—on how to smuggle things through, I suppose.
PAMELA (*laughing*) No, you idiot! Old-fashioned and out-of-date customs. (*Glancing at Hector quickly*) Like having butlers serving tea.
HECTOR. Now, now! That's too bad . . .
PAMELA. And I hope he makes a packet out of it. Then he might be able to take one of our stately homes himself with a butler of his very own. (*To Hector*) You'd like that, wouldn't you?
MORTIMER (*resenting the apparent friendliness between them*) It must be a nice easy life—being an author.
HECTOR. Well—it is and it isn't.
MORTIMER. But not much money in it, I should imagine.
PAMELA. *That* all depends, doesn't it?
MORTIMER. On what a chap writes, I suppose? If it's any good.
HECTOR. Maybe. Anyway—I don't believe that money is *everything* in life. (*He adds*) Even though I'm an American.
PAMELA (*anxious to avoid friction*) He's quite an idealist, isn't he, Mortimer?
MORTIMER (*coldly*) I'm afraid I prefer people to be practical.
PAMELA (*intervening quickly*) This is getting too deep for me. (*To Mortimer*) Have you seen mother and father yet?
MORTIMER. Your mother, yes, but I'm told that Sir George has (*with a smile*) disappeared.
PAMELA (*contritely*) Oh, yes. I was sent to look for him.

(*A door bangs off and* SIR GEORGE *is heard in a great state of excitement*)

SIR GEORGE (*off*) Caroline! Where are you? (*Shouting*) Caroline!
HECTOR. At a guess I'd say he'd found *himself*.
SIR GEORGE (*off*) Caroline! Caroline! Eh? Not you, Bellamy—your name's not Caroline, is it? No, you *can't* help . . . Run away, man— 'Pon, my soul, this is the *last* straw.

(*This is said as* SIR GEORGE *opens the double doors and comes stumping in*)

The last straw! Don't know what things are coming to . . . (*Turning to Hector*) Where's your mother?

HECTOR. Well, sir—I don't quite . . .

SIR GEORGE. Not *your* mother—*my* mother, I mean . . . (*Swinging to Pamela*) No, dammit, *your* mother. Where *is* she? This will upset her.

PAMELA. What on earth's happened, Father—anything serious?

SIR GEORGE. *Serious?* Should damn well think so. (*Suddenly bellowing across through the french windows*) *Caroline!*

(PAMELA *who is near to him, puts her hands over her ears*)

MORTIMER. She was here a moment ago.

PAMELA. Father, what's the matter?

SIR GEORGE. Matter enough, *I* can tell you.

MORTIMER. Let us into the secret, Sir George.

SIR GEORGE. It's no secret. It's all over the village. It's . . .

PAMELA (*very firmly*) Father!

SIR GEORGE. Eh, what?

PAMELA. Tell us in simple words what on earth you're talking about.

SIR GEORGE. Why, last night's burglary, of course!

PAMELA (*excited*) Burglary?

MORTIMER (*excited*) Not really?

HECTOR (*excited*) Where?

SIR GEORGE (*shouting; even more excited*) Keep calm, all of you—why can't you *keep calm?* (*He glares round*) It was at old Buster's. Hanley Close was burgled last night. I promised to ring Buster this morning about something, and he told me. So I went down right away to sympathize. It's scandalous!

PAMELA. It is rather alarming. (*To Mortimer*) That makes the third burglary in the last fortnight.

HECTOR. Say, it's getting quite like the States, isn't it?

MORTIMER. Not *quite,* I hope. I shouldn't be too worried, Sir George.

SIR GEORGE. But I *am* worried and . . . (*Apparently noticing him for the first time*) Hello, Mortimer. Where the devil have *you* sprung from?

PAMELA. He's been here all the time, Father.

SIR GEORGE. Why?

MORTIMER. You invited me for the week-end. I arrived just now.

SIR GEORGE (*pondering this before accepting*) Oh! So I did. (*To Mortimer, after a pause*) What d'you mean—"not to be worried"?

MORTIMER (*smiling*) Well—you're going on as if *you'd* been burgled. You haven't. *You're* all right. It's someone else.

SIR GEORGE (*after staring into space for a few seconds and then slapping his knee and bursting out laughing*) Gad! *That's* a point. Never thought of it that way. *I'm* all right. Thank you, Mortimer. Glad you're here to bring a bit of sense . . . (*Breaking off as he remembers*) Come to think of it, you're down here to talk over that little matter we discussed at the club, eh?

MORTIMER. That's it. As I told you, I've got a suggestion that may be helpful.

Sir George. Good. Let's get at it then. No time like the present. (*Leading Mortimer towards the door down* L) We'll go up to my study where we shan't be disturbed. Too many people here. Very distracting.

(Sir George *goes out down* L *taking* Mortimer *by the arm*)

Hector (*looking at Pamela*) I suppose that crack—too many people—was a hint for me to clear off?
Pamela. Oh, no. Just father. You'll get used to him.
Hector. I'd like to. He's—sort of unusual, but he's a good guy.
Pamela. We all adore him—even though we'd sometimes like to wring his neck.
Hector. And your mother—she's great, too.
Pamela (*laughing*) And also—sort of unusual?
Hector (*grinning*) You've said it.
Pamela. Perhaps we're *all* unusual.
Hector. *You* certainly are. (*Serious*) I thought that the moment I met you.
Pamela (*changing the subject quickly*) Anyway—Mortimer isn't.
Hector (*thoughtfully*) Y'know—I don't think he *cares* for me overmuch.
Pamela. What makes you think that?
Hector. Something in his manner—even allowing for his being English.
Pamela. I see.
Hector. Here—I shouldn't have said that, should I? No. I guess he could get along without my company quite a bit. (*He adds*) Not that it *worries* me any. (*Suddenly*) Here! I shouldn't have said that *either*, should I?
Pamela. If that's the way you feel—why not?
Hector. Because—well, I've got the idea that you and he . . . (*He hesitates*)
Pamela. We're not engaged, if that's what you mean. Not *yet*.
Hector. You mean . . . ? (*Again he hesitates*)
Pamela. We may be before the week-end's out.
Hector. But why on earth . . . ?
Pamela. Isn't that rather rude—or merely American?
Hector (*contritely*) Both I guess. I must apologize.
Pamela. Or—*explain?*
Hector (*shaking his head*) No, no. I've trodden in deep enough as it is. (*Suddenly changing his mind*) That is—unless you like a guy to be honest . . .
Pamela. I do. By the way, you thought you'd met Mortimer before, didn't you?
Hector (*swiftly*) Guess I was mistaken. Besides, that's not the point. I . . . Well, frankly, he doesn't seem your type—the sort of man a girl like you would fall in love with.
Pamela. How do you know I have?
Hector (*surprised*) But surely—if you're thinking of marrying the guy . . . ?

PAMELA. Then I must be madly in love with him?

(HECTOR *nods*)

That doesn't follow at all, these days. Quite a number of successful marriages have been based on much more practical things.

HECTOR. I don't see it that way, Pamela . . . (*He stops suddenly*) Say! I oughtn't to be calling you "*Pamela*", ought I?

PAMELA. Why not? You can if you like—*Hector*.

HECTOR. Thanks a lot. (*He smiles and continues seriously*) Well, I don't look at marriage that way at all.

PAMELA (*laughing*) You've seen too many of your Hollywood films.

HECTOR (*refusing to be sidetracked*) And I don't believe *you* do, either. So why do you have to put on this cynical act?

PAMELA. *Is* it an act? Or am I a little more grown-up than you imagine? I'm twenty-seven, you know.

HECTOR. What of that? I'm over thirty and I've been in love several times—pretty badly, too.

PAMELA. Well?

HECTOR. But never to the point of being *sure* enough to want to get married. Looks to me as if *you've* never been in love at all.

PAMELA. Haven't I? (*She turns away from him to hide her face*)

HECTOR. You mean . . . (*He hesitates*)

PAMELA. He was in the R.A.F. Killed in a crash—six years ago.

HECTOR (*softly*) Gee! That's tough.

PAMELA (*turning towards him again, her emotion past*) You get over these things, you know. You *have* to. You take what life still has to offer and make the best of it.

HECTOR. And that's why you're thinking of . . . ? (*He breaks off again*)

PAMELA. I've already told you—I'm twenty-seven. In three years I shall be thirty. Thirty! What else is there for a girl like me other than marriage? A spinster of this parish—getting older every year, heading for old-maidhood and entirely unfulfilled.

HECTOR. I don't see . . .

PAMELA (*interrupting him*) And I like Mortimer very much. We get on splendidly and I think he's very fond of me. There's not the slightest reason why we shouldn't be perfectly happy together.

HECTOR (*without conviction*) That's O.K. then. Fine. I'm sure you will.

PAMELA (*looking at him for a moment, as if realizing something*) And there's another thing that—that you must understand. I can't go out and make a living.

HECTOR. Why not—a bright girl like you?

PAMELA. Father'd be in the Bankruptcy Court and the place sold up within a couple of months without me to keep an eye on him. Dick has to be in London nearly all the time. And mother's hardly a tower of strength.

HECTOR (*laughing*) That last certainly is a British understatement. But (*looking puzzled*) this place—you don't mean Sir George is . . . ?

PAMELA. Hard up? He certainly is. And—it sounds terrible, I know—but Mortimer's pretty well off. That'll take care of things here.

HECTOR. I see. (*Thinking*) Yup, I see.

PAMELA (*lightly*) So that's how things are.

HECTOR (*looking steadily at her*) That's how things are.

(PAMELA *looks at him, seems about to say something else but turns away.*
BELLAMY *enters by the double doors*)

BELLAMY. Excuse me, miss, but cook is in need of your advice.

PAMELA. What's the trouble, Bellamy?

BELLAMY. The trouble is in the kitchen, miss.

PAMELA. Oh! Where's mother?

BELLAMY. In the kitchen, miss.

PAMELA (*smiling*) Ah, I understand. I'll come. (*To Hector*) Don't run away unless you have to. There are cigarettes somewhere. Bellamy will find them.

(PAMELA *goes out* LC. BELLAMY *takes the silver box of cigarettes from the table and offers it to Hector*)

HECTOR (*taking one*) Thanks.

(BELLAMY *offers him a light*)

Say, d'you mind if I have a little chat with you?

BELLAMY (*as he replaces the lid*) With *me*, sir? On what subject?

HECTOR. Butlers. Their life and work. For a book I'm writing on English customs. I guess a butler is by way of being a custom.

BELLAMY. An old and respected one, sir.

HECTOR (*taking out his notebook*) Miss Wareham tells me you were butler to three lords.

BELLAMY. That is so, sir. First to Lord Porteous and then . . .

HECTOR. Wait a bit! This Lord Porteous—were you with him long?

BELLAMY (*gravely*) Six months in the West End and then eight months in the prov—in his various houses up North, sir. Very good houses, too—particularly at York and Scarborough, I remember.

HECTOR. What was he like to work for?

BELLAMY. Work *with*, one could almost say, sir. He was extremely companionable off sta—off duty. When *I* was off duty, I mean. Believe it or not, sir, he was so companionable that he often condescended to borrow half a crown from me.

HECTOR (*making a note*) Say, that's nice to hear. (*Remembering Sir George and Lady Wareham*) Any odd ways about him—absent-mindedness or that sort of thing?

BELLAMY (*passing his hand over his mouth as he has his own little joke*) Yes, sir. Now you mention it—he had a habit of repeating himself every night.

HECTOR. You mean—saying the same thing?

(BELLAMY *nods*)

Every night?

BELLAMY (*gravely*) *Every* night, sir—and twice on Wednesdays and Saturdays.

HECTOR (*staring hard at him*) Say, you wouldn't be pulling my leg by any chance, Mr Bellamy?

BELLAMY. I wouldn't presume, sir. It is the simple truth. And—if I may be allowed to mention it—it would be better if you addressed me simply as "Bellamy". I speak entirely in the interests of decorum.

HECTOR. How's that again?

BELLAMY. Decorum, sir. The done thing.

HECTOR (*puzzled*) Well, anyway, it's friendly. But "Bellamy" without any "Mister" or anything sounds so kind of bald. Maybe I could call you by your first name?

BELLAMY. Butlers *never* have first names, sir.

HECTOR. Is that so? (*Puzzled again*) But here—how do they know at the christening that the baby's going to *be* a butler?

BELLAMY (*smiling*) Ah, there you have me, sir. I'm afraid I was too young at the time to remember.

HECTOR (*not quite sure if he is being fooled or not and deciding to attack*) Anyway—talking of names, that reminds me. (*Consulting his notebook*) All this funny spelling of English people's names. I've got a name down here that's spelled *Menzies* but seems to be pronounced "Mingies".

BELLAMY. That is a *Scottish name*, sir.

HECTOR. English—Scottish. Isn't it all the same?

BELLAMY. Some people think so, sir, but it's safer not to mention it too far north. In any case, "Mingies" *is* correct pronunciation, sir.

HECTOR (*referring to his book again*) And is Cahoon really the proper pronunciation of (*pronouncing it as spelt*) Colquhoun?

BELLAMY. Indubitably, sir.

HECTOR (*making a note*) Well—what d'you know?

BELLAMY. Another example you may care to jot down, sir, is (*spelling*) *Marjoribanks*.

HECTOR (*writing and pronouncing it as spelt*) Marjoribanks.

BELLAMY (*gravely*) No, sir. That one always puzzles American gentlemen. It is pronounced Chumley. (*He moves in a dignified fashion to the the double doors*) And Colonel Maltravers—of the recent burglary, you know, sir. His name is spelt (*spelling*) Buster.

(BELLAMY *goes out, leaving* HECTOR *staring after him, pencil poised and mouth open. Then he pulls himself together and laughs. Voices are heard off* LC, *those of* DICK *and* MAVIS)

DICK (*off*) I'll be with you in a second. I'll just take our mushrooms into the kitchen.

MAVIS (*off*) Right-ho!

(HECTOR *quickly puts away his pencil and notebook.*
MAVIS *comes in, shutting the french windows behind her*)

Oh! (*She is embarrassed at meeting a stranger*) Hullo!
HECTOR (*pleasantly*) Hello, there!
MAVIS (*realizing*) Oh—you must be what Dick calls Pamela's boyfriend.
HECTOR (*flustered, he has several answers to this one*) Well, I'd certainly . . . I mean, *she* doesn't . . . (*Collecting himself*) Well, not so's you'd notice.
MAVIS (*surprised*) But aren't you the Mr Mortimer Seaton who's coming here today?
HECTOR (*smiling*) No, I'm a different guy altogether—Hector C. Robson. I live near by.
MAVIS. Why, of *course!* The American! We were hearing a lot about you last night.
HECTOR. You mean the shooting affray?
MAVIS. That's right. I'm Mavis Montrose, by the way. I'm staying here.

(*Before Hector can reply,* DICK *enters by the french windows*)

Dick! Do you know who this is? *The* Mr Robson. One-gun Robson. (*To Hector*) Mr Richard Wareham.
DICK (*advancing*) Well! Well! Happy to meet you. Any fellow who shoots that horrible sister of mine is a pal for life.
HECTOR (*as they shake hands*) Glad to meet you, Mr Wareham.
DICK. I suppose you're visiting the wounded.
HECTOR. Yup. I—I was here with Pamela—don't mark me down as fresh—she asked me to call her Pamela—then she had to go some place and told me to wait.
DICK (*smiling at him in a friendly way*) Fine!
HECTOR (*looking from one to the other*) Perhaps . . . Guess I . . . Can I take a look round the garden?
DICK. By all means. I'll tell Pam.
HECTOR. Thanks.

(HECTOR *goes out through the french windows rather quickly*)

MAVIS. Wasn't that too sweetly tactful?
DICK (*laughing*) Yes. He seems a nice type. By the way, did you notice that Pamela stuff? Our friend Mortimer had better get cracking.
MAVIS. He's not exactly engaged to your sister, is he?
DICK (*smiling*) No more than we are, darling.
MAVIS. Oh.
DICK. What they call "an understanding". Official any moment. (*He puts an arm round her but she doesn't respond*) Anything the matter?
MAVIS. No. Of course not.
DICK. Sure?
MAVIS. Well—it's just—(*suddenly*) I wish your mother liked me more.

DICK. But she *does*.

(MAVIS *shakes her head*)

Well, she soon *will*. Mum always takes a little time to get "in gear" with strangers—if you know what I mean.

(MAVIS *nods*)

And don't you love this place?

MAVIS. It's heavenly. But it's—it's not quite what I'm used to.

DICK (*smiling*) No, it hasn't the glamour of London life exactly, I admit. But it's so lovely here in the country, and things seem so much more—*worth-while*, you'll find. I'm always looking forward to the time I can come and make a home here at last. (*Kissing her*) With you.

MAVIS. Darling!

DICK. And I'll tell you something—because your first marriage was an unhappy one, I'm all the more determined that the second one is going to make up for it.

MAVIS. You're very sweet to me. (*She lays her head on his shoulder briefly and then leaves him to turn away thoughtfully*)

DICK (*glancing at his watch*) Well . . .

MAVIS (*as if making up her mind*) Dick! Have you a moment?

DICK. Of course. But we've lots to do.

MAVIS (*sidetracked*) Lots to do?

DICK. Afraid *I* have. Masses of little jobs. I haven't been down here for over a month, you know, and dad isn't always—too efficient.

MAVIS. But he's sweet.

DICK. And it will be lovely having you come along with me while I do them. I want to show you *everything*. (*With mounting enthusiasm*) There's the stables and the horses and dear old Frost the groom—been with us for ages—(*imitating a country accent*) "Praper ole character, 'e do be." By the way, you *do* ride, don't you?

MAVIS. No, I'm afraid I don't know anything about horses.

DICK (*taken aback*) Good Lord! (*Recovering*) Oh, well, never mind! Bessie's got some new puppies, I'm told. You can play with them while I have a natter with Frost. Oh, and I must see Norgate, too.

MAVIS. Who's he?

DICK. Bailiff. Sort of estate sergeant-major. You'll learn a lot from him; and if we're going to be married soon you'll want to know about everything here as soon as possible, won't you?

(*During the above conversation* DICK *takes* MAVIS *by the arm towards the double doors*. MAVIS *releases herself, however, and stops*)

MAVIS. Darling! One moment—please!

DICK. What's up?

MAVIS (*in a low earnest voice, taking his hand*) Promise you won't be angry, darling, but there's something I must tell you.

DICK. You sound frightfully dramatic. What is it?

MAVIS. It's—it's about our being married.

DICK (*grinning*) If you're going to say you've changed your mind, I'll . . .

MAVIS (*smiling*) Don't be an idiot! (*Serious again*) It's just that we can't be married *too* soon, because (*with hesitation*) *actually* speaking my divorce isn't *quite* through yet.

DICK. I don't follow. I thought it was all over and done with and you hadn't seen your husband for two years.

MAVIS. I know. (*Unhappily*) I should have explained it at the start. But it's like this. We parted simply because we didn't get on together and I wanted to be free. And although I asked him he wouldn't agree to a divorce till I was certain there was somebody else I wanted to marry.

DICK. The selfish old So-and-so!

MAVIS (*hastily*) No, I think it was for *my* sake as much as for his own. He thought I might want to come back to him. And he promised me that if ever there *was* someone, he'd let me divorce him right away.

DICK (*brightening*) Hm! I see. Well, it needn't upset our plans, need it? It can't be long coming through now.

MAVIS. That's just it—it *may*. I wrote to him as soon as I knew about us, but he'd changed his address and I didn't get in touch with him for quite a while.

DICK. Oh, hell!

MAVIS. I'm sorry, darling.

DICK. Well, it can't be helped, I suppose. Things may sort themselves out sooner than you imagine.

(PAMELA *enters hurriedly through the double doors*)

PAMELA. Hello, you two! What's happened to my nice American?

MAVIS. He's looking at the garden.

PAMELA (*playfully imitating Hector*) Well, what d'you know? (*She crosses to the french windows, looks out and speaks a little anxiously*) I don't see him. He hasn't *gone*, has he?

DICK (*joining her at the window*) There he is! By the pond. (*Calling through the window*) Hi! Mr Robson, forward please! Customer needing attention. (*He returns, takes Mavis's arm and leads her towards the double doors*) We're going down to talk to old Frost. See you at lunch, Pam.

(DICK *and* MAVIS *go out* LC.
HECTOR *comes in through the french windows*)

PAMELA. Hector, I'm *so* sorry leaving you all this time. Knowing I was going to get involved with mother I should have told you not to wait.

HECTOR. That's O.K., Pamela. And you've got your—fiancé to look after, too.

PAMELA (*looking straight at him*) Yes. I have.

HECTOR. Then I guess I'll be pushing along. (*Slowly*) As a matter of fact I've got an important cable to send off.

PAMELA. Oh, dear! And I've kept you waiting.

HECTOR (*smiling and moving towards the double doors*) It didn't matter.

PAMELA (*on impulse*) Look! Why don't you come to lunch tomorrow?

HECTOR (*stopping; pleased*) Say, I'd just love to.

PAMELA. Splendid! Come soon after twelve, in plenty of time for a glass of sherry.

(LADY WAREHAM *comes hurrying in* LC)

LADY WAREHAM. Where's Richard? I want to ask him about these mushrooms. I'm quite certain most of them are toadstools. (*Suddenly finding she has nothing in her hands*) Now *what* have I done with the basket? (*Recognizing him*) Oh, good morning, Mr—er . . .

HECTOR. Robson. Good morning, Lady Wareham. And good-bye for the present. I'm just on my way.

(HECTOR *goes to the double doors accompanied by* PAMELA)

PAMELA. I've asked Hector to lunch tomorrow, Mother.

LADY WAREHAM (*raising her eyebrows*) Hector? Oh, yes, of course. (*She darts an annoyed look at Pamela, but her good breeding prevents her from speaking her own mind*) That will be *too* delightful. (*She favours Hector with a wan smile*)

PAMELA (*to Hector*) I'll see you to the door.

(HECTOR *and* PAMELA *go out* LC. *Alone,* LADY WAREHAM *again looks at her hands, as if expecting the basket to reappear, and then looks helplessly around the room.*

The door down L *opens and* MORTIMER *enters while* SIR GEORGE *is heard behind him*)

SIR GEORGE (*off*) . . . taxed the fella with being out shooting girls . . .

(LADY WAREHAM *makes an angry gesture.*
SIR GEORGE, *still talking, enters carrying an attaché-case*)

So I said "Girl over! Bang! Bang! Got her! Your girl, I . . . (*He breaks off as he sees Lady Wareham's face*)

(MORTIMER *laughs*)

Oh, sorry, m'dear. (*He puts his case down* R *of the desk*)

LADY WAREHAM (*icily*) Not at all, George. But I'm beginning to think Mr Robson must have had a repeating rifle.

(MORTIMER *again laughs, but* SIR GEORGE *doesn't get it and scratches his head in puzzled fashion.*
PAMELA *returns* LC)

PAMELA (*addressing Mortimer as she shuts the door*) Settled your business with father, whatever it was?

MORTIMER (*full of charm*) Not *settled* yet, is it, Sir George?

SIR GEORGE. No. Under serious consideration. (*To Lady Wareham*) Caroline, Mortimer's been putting a wonderful idea up to me.

ACT II BELLAMY 43

LADY WAREHAM. Well, after the ages you've been up there . . .

(PAMELA *joins* MORTIMER *and they chat together*)

SIR GEORGE (*interrupting*) Oh, we weren't discussing business all the time. We were talking about old Buster's burglary. Not so bad as it *might* have been, I suppose. Mortimer pointed out it wasn't *us*. (*Thinking*) All the same, it's all very well to say . . .

PAMELA (*coming across with Mortimer and interrupting*) Mortimer and I are going to look at Bessie's new babies. (*To Mortimer*) She's had four.

LADY WAREHAM (*aghast*) Bessie's had four . . . ? Oh, you mean Bessie the *sheepdog*. I thought for a moment . . . Yes, they *are* sweet. I don't suppose you'd care to buy one, Mortimer?

MORTIMER (*with his usual charm*) I'd love to, Lady Wareham, but I wouldn't really want a sheepdog in a London flat.

LADY WAREHAM. Why not? Oh, I see! You've no sheep, I suppose.

MORTIMER (*politely, but finding the charm difficult*) Exactly.

SIR GEORGE (*to Mortimer*) Better change those shoes if you're going to muck around the stable yard.

MORTIMER. It might be a good idea. (*To Pamela, as he starts for the double doors*) Shan't be long.

(*As he reaches the doors, they are opened by* BELLAMY *entering with a basket of mushrooms. He stands aside to let* MORTIMER *out.*

MORTIMER *exits* LC. BELLAMY *approaches Lady Wareham and coughs discreetly*)

LADY WAREHAM. Yes, Bellamy, what is it *now?*

BELLAMY. These mushrooms, m'lady. As you passed through the hall a short time ago you handed them to me, but omitted to specify what you wished done with them.

LADY WAREHAM (*after a moment's thought and smiling sweetly at him*) I've no idea.

BELLAMY (*resignedly*) Very well, m'lady. Then I will return them to the kitchen. (*He goes to the double doors and turns*)

(SIR GEORGE *turns and looks expectantly at him, awaiting the usual exit-line.*
But BELLAMY *goes out without saying a further word*)

SIR GEORGE. See that? He's gone without stopping at the door to say anything. What's he *mean*, sneaking out like that? (*To Lady Wareham*) Going back to what we were talking about. It's all very well for Mortimer to say don't worry about Buster being burgled. But it might be *us* next. Eh?

LADY WAREHAM. I can't imagine what that ridiculous village policeman is doing to let such things happen at all.

SIR GEORGE. *Collins*, you mean? He's doing his best—told us this morning it was an outside job.

LADY WAREHAM. What does that mean?

PAMELA. Someone broke in from outside.

LADY WAREHAM. *Surely* they couldn't come from anywhere else, could they?

SIR GEORGE. Yes. Might have been one of the servants. I mean to say—suppose it was *this* house, and Bellamy, or Pritchett, or the cook were to take our jewellery—well, that would be an *inside* job. See?

LADY WAREHAM. The idea's quite absurd! Why, all the servants have been with us for years. Except Bellamy, of course, and he's ... *Now* what's the matter, George?

SIR GEORGE. Good God! (*Suddenly plumping himself into the armchair with a horrified look on his face*) Supposing ... No, it *can't* be!

LADY WAREHAM. What *are* you talking about?

SIR GEORGE. Good heavens above!

PAMELA. Father! You don't mean you think Bellamy might be the *burglar?*

SIR GEORGE. Well—damn it all ... (*Scratching his head*) We were only saying yesterday there was something funny about him—those references and all that.

PAMELA (*slowly*) You mean he may have got this job under false pretences in order to *steal?*

SIR GEORGE. Been done before. And another thing—these thefts have all been since he came, haven't they?

PAMELA (*seriously*) I suppose it *is* an awful possibility.

SIR GEORGE. On the other hand, last night Bellamy was *here*, so he couldn't have been ...

LADY WAREHAM (*suddenly*) Oh! I've just remembered. Cook told me that after dinner he went down to the village.

SIR GEORGE. Ha! Or *said* he did!

LADY WAREHAM (*upset*) I can't believe it. Our own butler. Oh, dear, we shall all be burgled in our beds.

PAMELA. Don't be silly, Mother. We must think this over calmly and carefully and decide what to do.

SIR GEORGE (*rising and crossing to the phone*) I know what *I'm* going to do.

PAMELA. What?

SIR GEORGE. Send for Collins, of course, to come up and arrest him.

PAMELA. Steady, Father—you can't do that.

LADY WAREHAM. Why not, dear? I thought it was the usual thing if one found a burglar in one's house—even if the butler's one's own burglar—the other way round, I mean.

PAMELA. But we've no proof. It's only a *suspicion* on our part.

SIR GEORGE. That and forged references.

PAMELA. We can't be certain they *are* forged.

LADY WAREHAM. No. That Mavis girl said she *knew* the people and that Bellamy *had* been butler to them.

(SIR GEORGE *starts to dial his number*)

PAMELA. You see, Father. We don't know anything definite and you may land yourself in an expensive libel action.

Sir George (*hurriedly replacing the receiver*) Good Lord!
Lady Wareham. Wait! I've an excellent idea ... (*Beaming around*) Set a trap for him.
Sir George. Don't be absurd, Caroline. Fella's not a mouse.
Lady Wareham. Of course not. What I mean is ... (*To Pamela*) What *do* I mean, dear?
Pamela. Something like marked money left lying about to see if he takes it?
Lady Wareham. Yes. Or better still—jewellery. That's what the burglar took last night at Hanley Court.
Sir George (*enthusiastically*) Dashed good idea! And we'd better do it right away. Bellamy will be coming in soon with the morning coffee. If we leave a piece of jewellery on the table it may catch our man.
Pamela. I think you're overdoing things. And, anyway, I doubt if he'd be fool enough to swipe something so obviously left about.
Sir George. Then we mustn't make it too obvious. Here's an idea. (*Producing his attaché-case*) This has got my business papers—Stock Exchange, investment lists and so on. Put a bit of jewellery in *this*—where it might have got by accident—and see if he takes it.
Lady Wareham (*delighted*) That's *very* clever, George.
Pamela. *Personally*, my darlings, I think you're getting madder and madder!
Sir George (*opening the case*) Come on, Caroline. Give me something. That bracelet will do.
Lady Wareham. But I don't want it stolen. It's valuable.
Sir George. That's the whole idea. Who'd want to steal a thing that wasn't?
Lady Wareham. What about that diamond tiepin of yours, then?
Sir George. No, dammit! I don't want *that* taken. Something of yours.
Lady Wareham. Why not of yours?
Sir George. Because ... (*Struck by an idea*) By jove! I'd get the insurance money for it, wouldn't I? I could do with some ready money. (*He starts to take out his tie-pin*)
Lady Wareham. Oh, I never thought of that. (*Hurriedly taking off her bracelet*) That's different. (*She puts it into the attaché-case*)
Sir George (*putting in his tie-pin*) With luck he'll take both. (*He shuts the case*)
Pamela. Really, you two ...
Sir George (*interrupting*) Now we must fix a bit of cotton across the outside to know if it's been opened.
Pamela (*laughing*) Well, I suppose this is more harmless than ringing up the police. Here's a bit of cotton from mother's sewing. (*She picks it up from the settee*)
Sir George. Excellent. Excellent. (*Taking out his wallet*) And a bit of stamp paper to stick it on with. (*He sets his trap*)

(Lady Wareham *watches with interest*)

There! Now we're ready. (*Putting the case on the table*) We must all be out of the room. (*Leading the way*) Come on, Pamela.

(LADY WAREHAM *picks up the case*)

(*Turning and seeing her*) Good God, woman; don't *touch* it!
LADY WAREHAM. I thought I'd put my other bracelet in instead. It's insured for more money.
SIR GEORGE. Don't! If you do you'll break the cotton.
LADY WAREHAM. Oh! (*She replaces the case on the table*)

(PAMELA *bursts out laughing*)

SIR GEORGE (*rounding on her*) What's so funny?
PAMELA. *You*, my sweet! What does it *matter* proving the case has been opened, if the things are still there? And if they're *gone*, that'll prove it without all this cotton business.
SIR GEORGE (*staring owlishly at her*) You trying to make things difficult?
PAMELA (*throwing up her hands*) I give up!
LADY WAREHAM. I think you *should* when your father's being so *clever* about everything.
SIR GEORGE (*fussily moving the case to a new position on the table*) There! Quick now! We'll all go down to the end of the garden and wait.

(SIR GEORGE *propels* LADY WAREHAM *and* PAMELA *to the french windows and they go out*—PAMELA *having difficulty in controlling her laughter.*

SIR GEORGE *turns in the window opening, takes a last look at the case, grunts with satisfaction, turns up the collar of his jacket and follows them on tiptoe.*

After a short pause MORTIMER *comes into the room down* L. *He realizes that the others are probably in the garden and starts to go towards the window. As he does so he sees the attaché-case on the table. He pauses, casts a brief glance towards the door, looks out of the window and picks up the case. Then he opens it and examines the contents. He takes out the pin and bracelet casually, puts them down on the table and glances at the papers in the case. With the case in his hands, he goes again to the window and looks out. Then he begins to examine the papers in the case more carefully. He hears a jingle of cups off* LC, *shuts the case quickly and places it on the table.*

BELLAMY *enters with a tray-load of coffee and biscuits.* MORTIMER *breaks away from the table as* BELLAMY *carries the tray out on to the terrace and just out of sight down* R, *and then notices the pin and bracelet on the table by the case. But it is too late to do anything about it because* BELLAMY, *now standing just outside the window, picks up a handbell and rings it in the direction of the garden.*

BELLAMY *re-enters the room*)

MORTIMER (*as Bellamy returns*) Ah, the good old elevenses bell still in action, eh?
BELLAMY. Yes, sir. They will doubtless all be here in a moment.
MORTIMER (*indicating the jewellery*) It looks as if someone has been leaving valuables about.

BELLAMY. Dear me. So they have, sir.
MORTIMER. Hadn't you better take charge of them?
BELLAMY. Yes. Perhaps it would be wiser, sir. (*He picks up the tiepin and bracelet and puts them into his pocket*)

(MORTIMER *strolls out on to the terrace and off down* R.
BELLAMY *tidies the room. During this, voices are heard outside.*
SIR GEORGE, LADY WAREHAM *and* PAMELA *appear from the garden, go along the terrace and just out of sight down* R *for coffee.* BELLAMY *picks up Sir George's breakfast coffee-cup from the table by the desk and begins to move with it towards the double doors*)

SIR GEORGE (*off*) Shan't be a moment. Just remembered something I had to . . . (*He appears at the french windows and breaks off awkwardly as he sees Bellamy*) Oh! Ah! There you are, Bellamy.
BELLAMY. Yes, Sir George. (*He halts*)
SIR GEORGE (*edging to the table in an effort to get a better view of the attaché-case*) Yes, yes, there you are! Quite! (*Looking up*) Going, I see.
BELLAMY (*now at the door*) I was proposing to remove this cup to the back premises, Sir George.
SIR GEORGE (*anxious to be rid of him*) Yes, do, do!
BELLAMY. Thank you. (*Turning in the doorway*) I'm glad to have your full agreement on the matter, sir.

(BELLAMY *goes out* LC. SIR GEORGE *pounces on the attaché-case and examines it*)

SIR GEORGE (*vastly excited*) Broken, by jiminy! That settles it! (*Calling*) Caroline! I want you. Come here! Caroline!

(LADY WAREHAM *appears in the windows*)

It's broken, Caroline—broken by jiminy!
LADY WAREHAM (*coming towards the table*) Broken by *whom*, dear —and *what?*
SIR GEORGE. The cotton, of course. (*He opens the case*) Gone. Yes, by jove, he *has!* A moment earlier and I'd have caught him. This proves it! Up to the hilt! (*He bustles across to the phone, lifts the receiver and dials*)
LADY WAREHAM. What are you doing, George?
SIR GEORGE. Phoning the police, of course.
LADY WAREHAM. Dear me! It's just like a book!
SIR GEORGE (*into the phone*) That you, Collins? . . . Eh? Doesn't sound like your voice . . . Oh, that would account for it, I suppose, Mrs Collins. Get Collins. I've something to tell him . . . Out, is he? Where's he gone then? . . . Didn't ought to say? Really, Mrs Collins, this is Sir George Wareham speaking. I have most important news for him, and . . . Oh! What? . . . On his way to help arrest the burglar . . . ? Detective Inspector Blayde rang him? . . . Well, they're not here yet; I'm ahead of 'em. (*Chuckling*) I expect they'll be along any minute . . . What? I don't understand what I'm saying? . (*Getting angry*) Now look here . . . Oh, *you* don't. Really! Good-bye (*He puts*

down the receiver and turns to Lady Wareham) Silly woman says she doesn't understand what she's saying.

LADY WAREHAM. Neither do I.

SIR GEORGE. You didn't hear her.

LADY WAREHAM. I mean, I don't understand what *you're* saying.

SIR GEORGE. Now listen, Caroline! P.C. Collins and a Detective Inspector are on their way here to arrest Bellamy.

LADY WAREHAM. They can't possibly do that.

SIR GEORGE. Why not?

LADY WAREHAM. Because of lunch, of course.

SIR GEORGE. Dammit, don't you understand? He's the chap who bust Buster—who did all the other burglaries.

(*As he is saying this,* MAVIS *comes in through the double doors and stands listening.* SIR GEORGE *and* LADY WAREHAM *don't see her and proceed*)

LADY WAREHAM. But are the police certain Bellamy really *is* the burglar?

SIR GEORGE. Naturally. They wouldn't be on their way here to arrest him if they *weren't*, would they?

LADY WAREHAM. Yes, I see what you mean.

(*Upset and amazed,* MAVIS *goes silently out, closing the doors quietly behind her.*
PAMELA *appears at the windows from down* R)

PAMELA. Mother! Do you want me to pour the coffee?

LADY WAREHAM. What coffee? Oh, of course. No, dear. I'm just coming. (*She goes towards the windows*)

SIR GEORGE (*following*) How can you think of coffee at a time like this . . . By the way, where's *mine?*

LADY WAREHAM. I expect Bellamy is bringing it, dear.

(SIR GEORGE *and* LADY WAREHAM *go out on to the terrace.*
A second later BELLAMY *enters by the double doors. He carries a pint tankard—Sir George's "coffee"—on a salver. He starts moving gingerly across the room—obviously the tankard is very full and brimming over. After two brief halts, he shrugs his shoulders and solves the problem by raising the tankard to his lips and taking a short pull. He then moves rather quickly across and out through the windows. A moment later he returns with the salver. Suddenly he remembers the jewellery in his pocket, takes out tie-pin and bracelet and puts them on the salver.*
As he is about to return to the french windows, MAVIS *enters quickly* LC *and rushes to him. He turns*)

MAVIS. Trevor! Trevor!

BELLAMY (*glancing quickly over his shoulder towards the window*) What's up?

MAVIS. Oh, you fool! You *utter* fool! I knew from the first that you weren't being just a butler.

BELLAMY. But I am.

MAVIS. You're not. You're the burglar they're all talking about.

BELLAMY (*taken aback*) Me! Of course not.

MAVIS. I don't believe you. (*Pointing to the jewellery on the salver*) Why look!

BELLAMY (*angrily*) But you must believe me. It's absurd. It's . . .

MAVIS. Oh, never *mind!* Don't waste time lying to me—the police are coming to arrest you any minute.

BELLAMY. *What?*

MAVIS. They *are,* I tell you! I heard Sir George say so.

BELLAMY. To arrest *me?* But . . . but . . .

MAVIS. Here. Give me those. (*She snatches the bracelet and tie-pin from him*)

BELLAMY. But I was just going to return them to . . .

MAVIS (*crossing quickly*) Of course you were—now you're found out. (*Putting the bracelet and tie-pin on the mantelpiece*) I'll put them there and they'll turn up later. (*Returning to him and pushing him towards the door* LC) You must get away quickly—before the police come. I'll try and delay them or—tell them you've . . . Go to London. Have you enough money?

(*All this time* MAVIS *is pushing* BELLAMY *in the direction of the door and he is resisting her*)

BELLAMY (*acting a part quite unconsciously*) No, I'll stay and face this out—prove there has been a mistake—(*nobly*) I am innocent.

MAVIS. Stop acting, for God's sake! This isn't a scene out of *Falsely Accused.* This is *real!*

BELLAMY (*flustered*) I can't believe it. It can't happen. Life isn't like this.

MAVIS. It is. Oh, I know what you're thinking—someone will come rushing in to say they've arrested the real burglar or something. But this isn't your blasted stage.

(*The phone rings,* BELLAMY *goes to answer it. But* MAVIS *gets there first*)

No. I'll answer it while you get away. Quickly! Good-bye, my dear, and good luck. (*She picks up the receiver*)

(BELLAMY, *however, stands there dazed and then straightens up as if to face a firing squad*)

Hello! Yes! No, this is one of Sir George's guests. Did you want to . . . Yes, I'll take a message . . . (*She listens in mounting surprise*) Very well, I'll tell him. Thank you. (*She replaces the receiver and turns to Bellamy*) I—I just don't know what to make of it.

BELLAMY. Make of what? Who was it?

MAVIS. The police. To—to say they've arrested the burglar. He's been staying at a local inn, posing as an artist. Sir George is not to worry. *Not to worry!* (*She suddenly bursts out laughing*)

(BELLAMY *draws himself up, swelling with proud justification*)

BELLAMY. Now you see how right I was. Life is like the stage every time.

MAVIS (*suddenly serious again*) And I . . . (*Going to him*) Oh, Trevor, I'm so glad.

BELLAMY. You really thought I'd become a crook?

MAVIS (*nodding*) I'm—I'm awfully sorry.

BELLAMY. And yet you wanted to help me?

MAVIS (*a little near tears*) I suppose so—I—I—don't know—I . . . (*She gives a little sob*)

(BELLAMY *goes to her and takes her by the elbows*)

BELLAMY (*gently*) There! There! Don't work yourself up.

MAVIS. I—I can't help it! (*She suddenly buries her head on his shoulder, sobbing*)

(BELLAMY *pats her on the back with his other arm around her.*

At that moment DICK *enters by the double doors. Neither of them sees him.* DICK *pulls up short and starts to tiptoe out tactfully. Then the situation dawns on him and he swings round*)

DICK (*in angry surprise*) Bellamy!

(*They spring apart*)

BELLAMY (*politely*) You called, Mr Richard?

DICK (*quite flabbergasted*) I—I . . . Mavis, what on earth . . . ? (*Turning to Bellamy*) Bellamy, what the *hell* d'you think you're doing with this lady?

BELLAMY (*pulling himself up in a dignified way and speaking suavely*) That is no *lady*, sir. That is *my wife!*

Quick CURTAIN

ACT III

SCENE—*The same.*

When the CURTAIN *rises it is about a quarter to eleven the next morning and the sun is again shining brightly outside. The french windows are open and church bells can be heard faintly from a distance.* SIR GEORGE, *dressed for church in formal fashion, with his hat in one hand and a large hymnal in the other, is waiting with an air of martyrdom in the middle of the room. After a moment he puts his hat on the table, opens the hymnal and tries out one of the tunes, attempting to read the music and pom-pomming it. He makes a mistake and goes back with louder pom-pomming in an attempt to get it right.*

SIR GEORGE. Pom-pom-pom-*pom-pom!*

(*The door down* L *opens and* PRITCHETT *appear rather nervously*)

PRITCHETT. Is anything wrong, Sir George?
SIR GEORGE. Wrong? In what way?
PRITCHETT. I thought you called out.
SIR GEORGE. No. (*He resumes his pom-pomming*)

(PRITCHETT *interrupts, with some difficulty in gaining his attention*)

PRITCHETT. Shall I tell her ladyship you're in here, sir?
SIR GEORGE. Of course. I'm waiting for her. Where is she? We shall be late for church if she doesn't hurry up.
PRITCHETT. She's waiting for *you*, sir. In the hall.
SIR GEORGE (*annoyed, shutting the book and making for the double doors*) 'Pon my soul! I said I'd be *here*.

(*As he reaches the doors,* LADY WAREHAM *comes in hurriedly. They almost collide*)

LADY WAREHAM } (*together*) { Oh, there you are, George!
SIR GEORGE } { Oh, there you are, Caroline!

(PAMELA, MORTIMER *and* MAVIS *appear from the garden outside the windows on the terrace and watch the following*)

LADY WAREHAM. What *are* you doing here? I *told* you I'd be in the *hall*.
SIR GEORGE. You weren't when I came through just now.
LADY WAREHAM. No, I'd gone upstairs to see if you were *there*.
SIR GEORGE. Naturally I wasn't. I was *here* by then.
LADY WAREHAM. Oh, stop arguing and come along. (*She turns*) We shall be late.

(LADY WAREHAM *sweeps out* LC)

SIR GEORGE (*following*) Of course. Never been in time yet.

(SIR GEORGE *goes out* LC.

PRITCHETT *sees his hat on the table, grabs it and streaks out after them.* PAMELA, MAVIS *and* MORTIMER *enter by the french windows*)

PAMELA (*speaking to Mavis as they enter*) Believe it or not, we have that nearly every Sunday.

MAVIS (*smiling*) Really?

MORTIMER. It certainly happened on the week-ends I've been down.

PAMELA. I feel rather heathen at not going with them as usual.

MORTIMER (*winningly; meaning himself*) Ah, but you've got a guest to look after.

PAMELA (*smiling*) Three—if you include Dick. Though he's hardly ever in the house when he's here.

MAVIS (*looking at her watch*) That reminds me. I promised to meet him down at the stables, but I've a letter I simply must write first. (*She moves down* L) He wants to show me some young calves.

PAMELA. Don't let him turn you into a land-girl.

MAVIS (*without conviction*) Oh, but I like it.

(MAVIS *exits down* L)

PAMELA (*looking after her; reflectively*) You know, I wonder if she's the right person for Dick.

MORTIMER. Isn't she a mere passing attraction, then?

PAMELA. I'd say they were on the verge of getting engaged.

MORTIMER (*going to her and putting his arm round her*) Like us?

PAMELA (*unenthusiastically*) In a way—yes.

MORTIMER (*taking his arm away*) What's the matter, darling?

PAMELA. Why—nothing. (*She goes up to the window and turns. As she does so, she absent-mindedly touches the arm which was injured by Hector's shot*)

MORTIMER. That arm hurting you?

PAMELA. Eh? (*Removing her hand from her arm*) No, of course not. (*She comes to a decision and returns to him*) Mortimer dear! We've had an—what does one call it? An "understanding" for quite a while now.

MORTIMER. And I count myself a lucky man to have . . .

PAMELA (*holding up a hand to stop him*) What I mean is—(*smiling*) I'm being quite brazen about it, I'm afraid, but—don't you think we ought to get formally engaged now? (*Hastily*) I mean, if you really love me?

MORTIMER (*ardently, again putting an arm round her*) But, of course, I do.

PAMELA (*lightly; but with inner meaning*) Then you'd better make sure of me, hadn't you? There's no knowing *what* an unattached girl might take it into her head to do.

MORTIMER (*smiling*) But not *you!*

PAMELA. You'd be surprised. (*Without particular enthusiasm*) Anyway—let's tell father and mother it's definite.

MORTIMER. You mean—today—before I go back to London?

PAMELA. Why not?

MORTIMER. It's—it's a little difficult to explain. (*He is obviously wondering how to do it and removes his arm*) It's—it's this way. As you know. I'm down here specially to discuss some business with your father.
PAMELA. Yes. But what . . .
MORTIMER (*interrupting her*) I want him to take my advice, and if he does he should make quite a bit of money. But if I go to him and say I'm to be his son-in-law, he may think I'm offering to help him just to that end, and that my proposition isn't entirely disinterested. You see?
PAMELA. It seems rather muddled reasoning to me. However, the main point is clear—you don't want us to announce a formal engagement this week-end.
MORTIMER. It's not a question of *wanting*, darling. I'm thinking of what will benefit your father ultimately.
PAMELA (*suddenly smiling; quite changed*) Yes, I see what you mean now, Mortimer. Sorry I brought it up. Thanks for being so nice and thoughtful about everything. (*She briefly kisses him on the cheek and is away before he can respond*)
MORTIMER (*relieved*) That's all right. (*Looking out of the window*) I say, it's lovely out, isn't it? What about a walk?
PAMELA. Oh, Mortimer, I've such lots of things to do.
MORTIMER. Oh! All right!
PAMELA. You don't *mind* being deserted for a bit, do you? As you say, you didn't come down this week-end only to see me, did you?
MORTIMER. No, but . . . (*He breaks off*)

(BELLAMY *enters* LC *carrying some Sunday newspapers on a salver and also a small tissue-papered parcel*)

PAMELA. Ah, here are the papers at last. They get later and later each Sunday. (*She takes the top paper—"News of the World"—from the salver and gives it to Mortimer*) Here you are, Mortimer. You can have a nice quiet read in father's study till I'm free.
MORTIMER. All right, I will.

(MORTIMER *goes out down* L.
BELLAMY *places the other papers on the table and then turns and offers Pamela the parcel*)

BELLAMY. Here is the handkerchief, miss.
PAMELA (*taking the parcel*) Handkerchief?
BELLAMY. The one Mr Robson tied up your arm with, miss. You asked for it to be washed before you returned it.
PAMELA (*a little absently*) Did I? Oh, yes. Thank you, Bellamy. I'll give it to him at lunch. (*Struck with a thought*) No, I'm sure to forget. (*Casually*) I might as well walk down with it now—and we can come back together.
BELLAMY (*darting a quick look at her and then looking away and speaking drily*) That *would* be safer, miss.

(MAVIS *enters down* L. *She is carrying a stamped and addressed envelope*)

PAMELA. Oh, is that your letter, Mavis? Bellamy will put it in the box in the hall.

BELLAMY. Certainly, miss. (*He comes down and takes the letter from Mavis*)

(*As* MAVIS *gives it to him, she intimates at the same time that she wants to talk to him.* BELLAMY *goes to the table and starts rearranging the papers*)

MAVIS (*artificially bright*) I suppose I must go down and look at those calves soon. *You* won't be coming, will you, Pamela?

PAMELA. Heavens, no. (*Going to the doors* LC) We've been having calves here ever since I can remember and they all look alike to me. (*Laughing*) Except for the one essential difference.

(MAVIS *laughs too.*

PAMELA *goes out* LC. *The laugh then ceases abruptly as she rounds on Bellamy*)

MAVIS. Well, what have you to say for yourself?

(BELLAMY *shrugs his shoulders*)

You spoilt everything pretty nicely yesterday, didn't you?

BELLAMY. Did I?

MAVIS. Yes. Just because you couldn't resist trying to be funny with the old "That's no lady, that's my wife" gag.

BELLAMY. It wasn't *my* fault.

MAVIS (*angrily*) What?

BELLAMY. It was *his*. He gave me such a perfect cue.

MAVIS. Oh, I see! Well, you haven't done *yourself* any good, either. You can't stay on here as butler once his parents know you're legally my husband.

BELLAMY. All the same, I don't think your Dick will *tell* his parents.

MAVIS. Of course he'll tell them.

BELLAMY. Oh, no. Listen a minute. Dick wants to marry you, doesn't he?

MAVIS. Certainly he does.

BELLAMY. So he wants this divorce you let him think you'd already got?

MAVIS (*contritely*) I'm sorry about that. He knows now. I told him —yesterday.

BELLAMY. In your own words, I hope. Not (*dramatically*) "Promise me you won't be angry, darling?"

MAVIS. Of course I wouldn't be such a . . . (*Breaking off in confusion as she remembers*) Anyway—I told him.

BELLAMY. Right. And now he'll want to discuss the whole matter with me face to face. But if he spills the beans to dad and mum I'll be out on my ear in a flash and everything will be much more difficult to arrange. See?

MAVIS. Yes, I suppose there's something in that. (*Turning away*) Oh, what a mess!

BELLAMY. Cheer up. It'll all come out in the end. Wedding bells for you; and for *me* . . .
MAVIS (*cutting in a little bitterly*) A heavy self-sacrifice act in a pale pink floodlight. (*Contritely*) I'm sorry. I shouldn't have said that. Or were you *really* hoping I'd come back?
BELLAMY. Only up to the time you found someone else.
MAVIS (*sitting in the armchair*) Trevor, dear, I'm sorry I couldn't make a go of our marriage. I *did* try—honestly. But the whole thing was a mistake. It ought never to have happened in the first place.
BELLAMY. I don't see why not.
MAVIS. Oh, yes, you do. That blasted tour up North—going on and on—was really what did it. And you being so different from the other men in the show. It was—well, just proximity.
BELLAMY. *And* the fact that I was really in love with you.
MAVIS. *Were* you?
BELLAMY (*nodding*) But you weren't with me.
MAVIS (*considering*) Perhaps I was. Till you refused to get on—and assert yourself.
BELLAMY. As you said—content with butler parts.

(DICK *comes in through the french windows, from the garden*)

DICK. Ah, there you are, Mavis! (*Halting as he sees Bellamy*) Oh! Excuse me!
BELLAMY (*respectfully*) Not at all, sir—excuse *me*. (*He bows and begins to move to the double doors*)
DICK (*hastily*) No, don't go. We three simply must get all this sorted out.
BELLAMY. Just as you wish, Mr Richard, sir.
DICK (*awkwardly*) Now look here, Bellamy. Cut the butler stuff for a bit, will you? Mavis has told me about you. Now—let's pretend we're meeting on common ground somewhere—at a club, for instance.

(BELLAMY *bows gravely, pauses and then suddenly sits down in a chair* R *of the table, crosses his legs and speaks in his own voice*)

BELLAMY. O.K., old boy. Let's have it out. (*Picking up the cigarette box and offering it*) Smoke?
DICK (*embarrassed and then recovering quickly*) No, thanks.
BELLAMY. Right you are. (*He takes a cigarette himself and lights it*)
DICK (*watching him*) Well—that's certainly better. (*He sits at the table*) Now I'll put my cards on the table. As you know, Mavis and I want to get married. (*He pauses*)

(MAVIS *brings the desk chair to the table and sits*)

BELLAMY (*easily*) Carry on.
DICK. When you separated you promised her a divorce as soon as she wanted one.

(BELLAMY *nods*)

You're still prepared to honour that?

BELLAMY. I promised, didn't I? That is enough. If I lose mine honour I lose myself. Hrm! *Antony and Cleopatra*.

MAVIS. Stop *acting*, Trevor.

BELLAMY. I wasn't acting. I was quoting. (*To Dick*) It's really up to Mavis. (*To Mavis*) *You* want it?

MAVIS (*after a slight hesitation*) Y-yes.

BELLAMY. Then that settles it. I'll start things going. (*To Mavis*) Do *you* wish to be the guilty party, or . . .

DICK (*interrupting him quickly*) Of course she doesn't. What are you thinking of?

BELLAMY. Act two, Scene two of *The Great Decision*.

(*This brings a reaction from* DICK)

Now don't get angry, my dear fellow. I only want to know exactly how I stand.

DICK (*firmly*) *You* provide the evidence—that is, if you don't mind, I mean.

BELLAMY. Not at all, old boy. I understand exactly.

MAVIS. Trevor dear, it *is* sweet of you.

DICK. Yes, Trev—I mean, Bellamy. We're extremely grateful. Oh, by the way, I'm naturally not telling my people about this.

BELLAMY. I quite understand. (*Sadly*) All the same, it doesn't look as if I shall be able to stay on here, does it?

MAVIS. It seems a shame—but I suppose you can't possibly.

BELLAMY. Too awkward all round. Besides, I might forget my lines. (*To Mavis*) Suppose while serving you with sherry, I said, "Or would you rather have a Guinness, dear—I know you prefer it"?

MAVIS (*laughing*) How right you'd be. Remember those awful digs we had at Sheffield where the landlady's small boy . . .

DICK (*cutting in a little coldly*) Yes, quite, quite! (*To Bellamy*) I'll certainly see you get the best references my parents can give.

BELLAMY. That's jolly decent of you, old man.

DICK. Not at all, old man. Jolly decent of *you* to be so co-operative.

BELLAMY. Glad to oblige, old man.

(SIR GEORGE *comes in* LC. *He moves behind the chair on which Bellamy is seated and so* BELLAMY *does not notice him. Neither does* SIR GEORGE *know it is Bellamy in the chair*)

SIR GEORGE (*crossing behind the chair*) Ah, hello, Dick!

(BELLAMY *realizes who it is but, as* SIR GEORGE *now turns to him, he does not have time to get up, only to whip out a handkerchief and blow his nose loudly, thereby concealing his face from* SIR GEORGE, *who doesn't immediately recognize him.* SIR GEORGE *addresses him awkwardly, as to a stranger*)

Ah, how d'you do? (*He turns to Dick and speaks in a loud whisper*) Who's your friend? Introduce me, dammit!

(*The moment Sir George's back is turned,* BELLAMY *jumps up, moves swiftly to the double doors and stands there as if he had just entered*)

DICK (*hustled*) My—my friend?
SIR GEORGE. Yes. (*Jerking his thumb over his shoulder towards the now-empty chair*) Chap sitting there. (*Annoyed at Dick's "goldfish" goggling*) Where are your manners? (*He turns back and his mouth falls open as he sees the empty chair*)

(MAVIS *and* DICK *are now reacting in amusement.* SIR GEORGE'S *eye now roves round the room till it rests upon* BELLAMY *who is politely waiting by the door*)

BELLAMY. Did you ring, Sir George?
SIR GEORGE (*flabbergasted*) Ring? Me? What for?
BELLAMY. It was upon that very point I was seeking information, sir.
SIR GEORGE. Yes, but . . . (*Rounding on Dick*) Where's the fella who was there?
DICK (*hiding his amusement*) Fellow, Father?
SIR GEORGE. Yes. Fella, fella, fella! Sitting in that chair. Thought he was a friend of yours. Where's he *gone?*
MAVIS (*also struggling with laughter*) *Was* there anyone, Sir George?
SIR GEORGE. Why, you damn idi . . . (*Reacting*) Hrmf! Sorry, m'dear. Thought I was speaking to Dick.
BELLAMY (*suavely*) If I may venture the suggestion, sir, it was probably a trick of the light—a reflection from the mirror there on to the chair opposite Mr Richard sitting in *his* chair.
SIR GEORGE (*scratching his head and staring at the empty chair*) Mirror! Trick of the light! Don't understand.
BELLAMY (*opening the double doors*) If there is nothing further, Sir George, I will return to my *own* reflections.

(BELLAMY *goes out* LC)

SIR GEORGE (*rounding on Dick and Mavis*) Now look here, you two . . .
DICK (*quickly*) You're back from church awfully early, aren't you, Dad?
SIR GEORGE (*sidetracked*) Ha! Yes. (*Triumphantly*) Matter of fact, we came out as soon as it started. Vicar's laid up again and that chap from Lower Parton was taking the service. *Awful* fella—always preaching sermons against the rich in general and looking at me in particular. Wouldn't mind if I *was* rich, but in my case it's an insult. Here, that reminds me. I want to have a chat with Mortimer. Where's he got to?
DICK. Haven't a clue. With Pam somewhere I shouldn't wonder.
SIR GEORGE. Ah, yes, of course. (*He starts for the double doors*)

(*They open to admit* LADY WAREHAM)

LADY WAREHAM. Have the papers come yet?
SIR GEORGE (*indicating them*) There they are on the table! Unless it's a trick of the light. (*He goes out,* LC)
DICK. Come on, Mavis. Those calves.

(DICK *and* MAVIS *exit* RC. LADY WAREHAM *crosses* L *and rings the bell and then begins to search through the papers.*
After a pause BELLAMY *enters*, LC)

BELLAMY. You rang, m'lady?
LADY WAREHAM. They've forgotten to send the *News of the World*, Bellamy.
BELLAMY. Tut, tut! Perhaps you would care to peruse my personal copy?
LADY WAREHAM. No, thank you. (*Taking up a paper*) The *Sunday Times* will do just as well. (*Struck by a new thought*) You know, Bellamy, I'm awfully glad you're still here.
BELLAMY. I wasn't aware that I had ever been going, m'lady.
LADY WAREHAM. All the same, you nearly *went*. Police Constable Collins had some stupid idea you were mixed up in all those burglaries.
BELLAMY. Indeed, m'lady?
LADY WAREHAM. Surely you knew? But Sir George phoned him and told him not to be such an idiot. (*After thinking*) Or was it Collins who phoned Sir George and told him not . . . (*Hastily*) Anyway, it's all right now.
BELLAMY. I was certain it would be, m'lady.
LADY WAREHAM (*interested*) How could you be *certain?*
BELLAMY. I have had considerable experience of the . . . of life, m'lady. I remember once when I was in . . . when a certain Mr Robin Goodheart, for whom Miss Marjorie Carstairs, the daughter of my then employer, had an obvious affection, was actually discovered shortly after midnight, standing by an open safe from which valuables had recently been removed.
LADY WAREHAM. Goodness!
BELLAMY. Despite his statement that he had heard a noise and merely came to investigate, he and he alone appeared to be the thief—particularly so as he was suffering from desperate financial embarrassment. Fortunately a clever piece of detection resulted in . . .
LADY WAREHAM. You mean there was a detective in the house?
BELLAMY. Oh, *no*, m'lady. When a real detective happens to be one of the week-end house party, one can confidently anticipate a murder in the library quite early on.
LADY WAREHAM. No! Really?
BELLAMY. Indeed, yes. Usually connected with the somewhat eccentric provisions of a missing will.
LADY WAREHAM (*much impressed*) Dear me, Bellamy. What a lot of useful things you know.
BELLAMY (*bowing gravely*) Thank you, m'lady. The detective in this case was an amateur—a high-spirited cousin of Miss Marjorie's who wore a monocle and until then had been looked upon as a mere buffoon.
LADY WAREHAM. Buffoon?
BELLAMY. Definitely. *But* a mere cloak for a very keen intelli-

gence. He was somewhat inadequately assisted in his deductions by Charles.

LADY WAREHAM. Charles?

BELLAMY. Charles, his friend, m'lady.

LADY WAREHAM. Oh! But who had done it then?

BELLAMY. The guilty person turned out to be a Sir Jasper Crookshank, to whom Miss Marjorie was engaged to be married, although —as I have intimated—her affections were really bestowed elsewhere.

LADY WAREHAM. Why was she engaged to him, then?

BELLAMY. He was rich, and her father, to whom she was devoted, was not well off. Moreover, Sir Jasper had secured, through an intermediary, a mortgage on his host's ancestral home and was threatening to turn them all out on what—if I remember correctly —was a particularly snowy night.

LADY WAREHAM. Oh dear!

BELLAMY. He had also engineered the robbery in an unsavoury attempt to throw suspicion on Mr Robin, his hated rival in the lists of love.

LADY WAREHAM. Dear me, what an unpleasant person!

BELLAMY. Indeed, yes, m'lady. Though it was not apparent till near the end when he was unmasked.

LADY WAREHAM (*almost spellbound*) Then what happened?

BELLAMY. Sir Jasper was dismissed the house and Miss Marjorie immediately accepted the attentions of Mr Robin.

LADY WAREHAM. How unwise! If he was so impecunious, I mean.

BELLAMY (*smiling gravely*) Ah, yes, m'lady. But it was subsequently discovered that he was, in fact, extremely rich and had only pretended to be poor, lest his wealth might unduly influence the object of his affections.

LADY WAREHAM (*delighted*) Go on. Tell me more.

BELLAMY. There is little more to recount, m'lady. The course of true love ran smooth. I think Miss Marjorie's last words were: "Can you ever forgive me for suspecting you?"

LADY WAREHAM (*alarmed*) Last words! Surely you don't mean ...

BELLAMY. The last words *I* heard her say, m'lady. It was the curtain.

LADY WAREHAM. The what?

BELLAMY. It was *certain* they would be happily married.

LADY WAREHAM. Oh, I see. Really, Bellamy, you've been most interesting—and helpful.

BELLAMY. I endeavour to give satisfaction, m'lady. (*Going to the doors* LC *and turning*) Any time you may need advice my experience has been such that I am generally able to offer a solution.

(BELLAMY *goes out through the double doors.*
SIR GEORGE *comes in from the garden in time to witness his exit*)

SIR GEORGE. There he goes again—never going out without *saying* something.

LADY WAREHAM. All the same, George, I've come to the conclusion Bellamy is a most remarkable man. His knowledge of life is most—er—expansive. I have a very good mind to ask his advice about Pamela.

SIR GEORGE. What's she done?

LADY WAREHAM. A little while ago I saw her walking down the drive alone—*and*, I suspect, in the direction of that Mr Robson's cottage. In fact, I think she's getting too fond of him.

SIR GEORGE (*startled*) What? Nonsense. Can't be. She's engaged to Mortimer.

LADY WAREHAM. Not *yet*, George. And I shall be most relieved when she *is*. You know what girls are. It would be nothing short of a disaster if she changed her mind.

SIR GEORGE. You mean gave Mortimer the go-by? Terrible! (*Thoughtfully*) Of course this Robson fella's not a bad type. Rather took to him—in a way.

LADY WAREHAM. George, have you no sense at all? For one thing he hasn't any money.

SIR GEORGE. Nor have *we*—(*hastily*) I mean—how do you know that?

LADY WAREHAM. He wouldn't be living in that poky little cottage trying to scrape a living writing if he had. And what's his father? A builder in a small American town apparently—he was very evasive about it. Probably only a bricklayer if the truth were told. He admitted that his "pop" was a "man of the people".

SIR GEORGE. See what you mean—yes. Never thought of it like that.

LADY WAREHAM. Then it's time you did. Hardly the sort of son-in-law to help you with your roofs and so on, like Mortimer could.

SIR GEORGE. Good Lord, no. I mustn't lose Mort . . . I mean *she* mustn't lose Mort . . . I mean, she'd be *happier* with Mortimer, wouldn't she? (*Suddenly*) There's that ready-money problem, too—thing he's advising me about. (*Going*) Think I'd better find him and get it settled—just in case y'know—just in case.

(SIR GEORGE *goes off* LC. *Left alone*, LADY WAREHAM *is about to start doing something indefinite with great intensity.*

DICK *comes in through the window, carrying* MAVIS *in his arms*)

LADY WAREHAM. Good heavens, Dick! *Don't* say Mr Robson has been out shooting again?

DICK. It's all right, Mum. It's only her shoe. (*Putting her down*) Heel's come off. (*He holds it out*)

LADY WAREHAM (*taking it*) How annoying. (*Examining it*) It *is* rather a high one, isn't it?

MAVIS. I'm afraid all my heels are rather high—for the country, that is.

LADY WAREHAM. We must get it mended for you. What a pity it's Sunday. (*Suddenly*) Never mind! Bellamy! Perhaps *he* can do it. He's so clever about *everything*.

(LADY WAREHAM *goes fussily off* LC *with the shoe and heel*)

DICK. What a stupid thing to happen—just when I wanted to . . .

MAVIS (*interrupting rather crossly*) It's all very well to say that. You're used to stables and cobbled yards and climbing into lofts and things. I'm *not*.

DICK. Good Lord, darling—this *is* the country—not Shaftesbury Avenue.

MAVIS (*coldly*) That *has* dawned on me. (*Looking at a ladder in her stocking*) And I've ruined my best pair of nylons as well.

DICK. I can't understand why you didn't bring some more sensible things with you.

MAVIS (*emotionally*) Can't you? Well, I haven't *got* "more sensible things" down here. I wanted to look my best—to meet your people and . . .

DICK. I dare say, but . . .

MAVIS (*with a slight sob*) I wanted to do you credit and . . .

DICK (*going to her and putting his arms around her*) But you always *do* do me credit. Whenever we go into a restaurant everyone turns to look at you . . .

MAVIS (*naïvely; cheering up*) Do they really? (*Thoughtfully*) But London isn't here.

DICK. No, thank heaven. (*Squeezing her*) This is so much more *real* than London. The country always is.

MAVIS. Is it?

DICK (*surprised*) Of course. It's *life*. London's only *fun*. Don't worry, darling, you're going to have lots of time to get used to it.

MAVIS (*slowly*) Yes. Yes, I suppose I am.

DICK. All your life, my sweet. (*He raises her head and kisses her*)

(BELLAMY *comes in through the double doors carrying the mended shoe*)

BELLAMY (*coughing discreetly*) Ahem!

(*They break apart*) Dear me, yet *another* familiar situation—husband enters unexpectedly to find wife . . .

MAVIS. Oh, Trevor—for heaven's sake!

BELLAMY (*crossing*) Your shoe, miss. (*He gives it to her*)

(MAVIS *sits* R *of the table to put it on*)

DICK. You've been jolly quick.

BELLAMY. Merely a matter of a couple of nails and a hammer, sir.

DICK. Here, I say—don't start being a butler with us again.

BELLAMY. It would be safer if I sustained the role throughout, sir. "Doubling a part" is apt to lead to confusion sometimes. (*Indicating the chair in which he sat previously*) You may recollect your father entering just now.

MAVIS. I think he's right.

DICK. Suppose so.

BELLAMY (*bowing gravely*) Thank you, sir.

DICK. You know, Bellamy, I really wish you were staying on. You're the best butler we've ever had.

MAVIS. But he can't possibly.

BELLAMY (*smiling and bowing again*) Quite. (*To Dick*) I must confess that I should *like* to remain with you, sir—if only to observe how the young lady settled down as a member of the family.

DICK. She'll settle down all right, don't you worry.

BELLAMY. Oh, I'm not *worrying*, sir. She has always been able to make the best of things.

DICK (*not quite liking this*) She won't have to "make the best of things" here.

BELLAMY. Indeed no, sir. I'm sure she'll be most happy. Already I visualize her helping with the W.I. and other village activities.

MAVIS (*apprehensively*) The W.I.?

DICK. Women's Institute. A kind of regular get-together of all the village women. Mum's president again this year.

MAVIS (*doubtfully*) Oh—I see.

BELLAMY (*to Mavis*) You'll find it most stimulating. My own mother was tremendously keen about it, I recollect. They used to have lantern lectures and competitions for cake-making and embroidery. Or lessons in basket-weaving and the making of soft toys.

(MAVIS *looks at* DICK, *who smiles reassuringly*)

MAVIS (*more doubtfully*) I'm afraid it's not *much* my line.

BELLAMY. Ah, but it will *have* to be! (*To Dick*) Won't it, sir? (*To Mavis*) And you'll have lots of other pleasant things to do. (*With a look at Dick*) Riding and so on.

DICK. Yes, of course. She's . . . (*With a change of tone*) Here! You know jolly well she doesn't ride.

BELLAMY (*with feigned surprise*) But I have seen her sitting on a horse to the manner born.

MAVIS (*sharply*) Nonsense! I've always been *terrified* of . . . I mean —where was this?

BELLAMY. On the Central Pier at Blackpool.

DICK (*startled*) Pier?

BELLAMY. Yes, sir. If I remember correctly my *own* mount was an ostrich.

DICK. Stop being an idiot, Bellamy, I'll teach her to ride soon enough.

MAVIS (*in a small voice*) That'll be lovely.

DICK. I mean to say—one simply *has* to be in with the hunting crowd around here.

MAVIS (*aghast*) Hunting! I could *never* do that. (*She rises and moves down* R)

DICK. But damn it all . . .

BELLAMY (*interrupting*) You must be patient, sir. I have no doubt she'll be a grand rider to hounds. In time, of course, and after a few tumbles.

(MAVIS *and* DICK *look uneasily at each other and then away*)

Now regarding this divorce. I presume my first task is to look around for a suitable co-respondent.

DICK. Oh, that's all a formality. Just a hotel bill and a chambermaid as a witness and . . .

BELLAMY (*holding up his hand*) Excuse *me*, sir. Collusive evidence is illegal—and dangerous. We mustn't run the risk of the divorce not going through. No, it must be done properly.

MAVIS (*apprehensively*) Trevor! You surely don't mean you're really going to . . . (*She breaks off in confusion*) I mean, do you?

BELLAMY. I feel it my duty—and it may not be *too* distasteful. (*Getting ideas*) Yes. *Yes*. (*Briskly*) Mavis, what was the name of that pretty little redhead who was with us in *Desert Passion?* Petronella something? Are you still in touch with her?

MAVIS (*curtly*) Yes. And you're not going to be.

BELLAMY. Pity.

DICK. Look here, Mavis. You asked him for the divorce. How he goes about it is entirely his own affair.

BELLAMY. Entirely. (*He smiles at Mavis*)

(MAVIS *gives him a furious look*)

DICK (*suddenly looking at his watch*) Here, I've already kept Norgate waiting twenty minutes. I've got to go. (*Moving* LC) I don't suppose you want to risk your shoes again, Mavis, do you?

MAVIS. I'd rather not, thanks, Dick. (*Slowly*) And I've a feeling there are a few things you may not want to risk after all, either.

DICK. Eh? Perhaps. I hardly know.

(DICK *goes out* RC *looking very thoughtful.* MAVIS *watches him go, then turns and faces Bellamy in silence for a moment*)

MAVIS. Trevor! I've got something serious to say to you.

BELLAMY (*in his normal voice*) O.K. Fire away!

MAVIS. It's like this . . .

(*The telephone rings*)

Oh, blast the thing!

BELLAMY (*crossing, lifting the receiver and speaking in his "butler" voice*) Barwell Towers . . . Yes, it's the butler . . . What? . . . A call from Florence? Florence who? Where are your manners, young woman? . . . What? (*He rocks slightly and gulps*) Name of a town? But that's in *Italy!*

MAVIS. Good heavens!

BELLAMY (*into the phone*) What do you mean "*You* say"? I didn't say anything . . . (*Quite overcome*) Wha-what? . . . U.S.A.? (*He looks helplessly at Mavis*)

(MAVIS *is equally astonished*)

Florence, South Carolina, U.S.A. . . . A Mr Xerxes J. Robson is calling? . . . All right, I'll hold on.

MAVIS (*sinking into the armchair*) Well! (*Sitting up suddenly*) It must be Hector Robson's father.

BELLAMY. Couldn't be anyone else.

MAVIS. But ringing up from America? *Why?*

BELLAMY. Probably wants to find out what his son's up to. (*Suddenly*) Here! Quick! I've an idea. I'm pretty sure young Robson and our Pamela have fallen for each other in a big way. We may be able to lend a hand.

MAVIS. How?

BELLAMY. Remember how in *Love's Young Dream* the unknown little shopgirl turned out to be the Hon. Claire Montmorency?

MAVIS. Don't be absurd. What's that got to do with ...

BELLAMY (*into the phone*) Yes, I am continuing to hold the line. (*To Mavis; still excited*) We've got to help this thing on. Impress Hector's father and make him think his son's in with the top-drawer nobs. (*Holding out the receiver*) Here! Grab this!

(MAVIS *hesitates*)

Quick! You're the maid! (*He pushes the receiver into her hands*)

(MAVIS *refuses it*)

Or aren't you a good enough actress?

MAVIS. Oh—all *right!* (*Taking the receiver*) If you're determined to turn the whole world into your own private stage ... (*She breaks off and then speaks into the receiver in a slightly common "maid" voice*) Yes, Barwell Towers ... Oh, no, this is the maid.

BELLAMY (*prompting*) One of the maids!

MAVIS (*into the receiver*) One of the maids ... Who? ... You're sekketry to Mr Robson? ... Yes, miss ... No, I couldn't say, I'm shore, miss. But the butler's 'ere. Perhaps you'd care to speak to him.

BELLAMY (*taking the receiver from her*) Good! (*Speaking into the phone*) The butler here, miss. Is there anything ... Mr Xerxes Robson wishes to speak with Mr Hector Robson? ... But this is Sir George Wareham's residence ... Oh, I see. Call transferred from Elm Tree Cottage? In that case I'd better put you through to Sir George in person. I think he's in the brown study conferring with the archbishop ... Oh, yes, his Grace always comes on Sundays to take Sir George's private service. Will you be good enough to hold on a moment? (*He makes a clicking sound with the receiver and hands it to Mavis*)

MAVIS. What—me again?

BELLAMY. You're Sir George's private secretary. Jump off his knee and answer.

MAVIS (*speaking into the receiver; very "refaned" indeed*) Sir George's pravate secretary. Kin aye help you ... Ay'm afraid I don't know where Mr Robson Junior *is*. (*Looking helplessly at Bellamy*) He's expected to lunch, I know.

(BELLAMY *whispers in her ear*)

(*She stares at him in amazement*) You'd—better speak to Sir George himself.

(*With a broad grin,* BELLAMY *takes the phone, squares his shoulders and speaks into it in imitation of Sir George*)

BELLAMY. Hey, what? What's that? I mean, *who's* that? ... Mr Xerxes J. Robson wants to speak to me? Well, here I am! Put him him through, young woman, put him through ... Eh? What? ... Oh, hullo! ... Morning! What can ...

(*During the above dialogue* SIR GEORGE *enters from down* L. MAVIS, *aghast, wildly tries to attract Bellamy's attention, but* BELLAMY *shrugs her away. Then suddenly* SIR GEORGE *comes into view and he breaks off flabbergasted*)

SIR GEORGE. Did I leave my fountain-pen here? (*To Bellamy*) Why are you talking in that damn silly voice, Bellamy?

(BELLAMY *opens and shuts his mouth helplessly*)

You sound quite idiotic! Who's the call for? (*He takes the receiver*)
BELLAMY (*hustled*) It—it was for Mr Hector Robson.

(SIR GEORGE *looks puzzled*)

He's expected to lunch, but has not arrived yet.
SIR GEORGE. Oh, yes, of course. (*Into the receiver*) Sorry, he's not here yet. Will you ring later? (*He is about to replace the receiver*)
BELLAMY (*in a strangled voice*) Allow me, sir! (*He manages to take it from him just in time*)
SIR GEORGE. Now, fountain-pen? (*He finds it in his pocket*) Ha! Here it is all the time. (*He crosses back to the door down* L) I'm busy in the study with Mr Seaton. Don't disturb me again.

(SIR GEORGE *goes out down* L. BELLAMY *produces the receiver from behind his back and speaks into it as Sir George again*)

BELLAMY. Are you still there, Mr Robson? . . . Ah, so glad! . . . Must apologize. Some damn fool came into the room. Any message I can give your son? . . . Oh, concerns me really, does it? (*He glances towards Mavis and listens attentively*) Yes, quite understand . . . Not really? . . . Good heavens . . . You're quite sure of that? . . . No, no, no. 'Course you wouldn't . . . Well, well, well, well! . . . Well, this is a . . . No, extremely good of you to let me know . . . Obliged to you . . . Most grateful . . . Yes, yes. 'Bye . . . 'Bye. (*He puts down the receiver and faces Mavis with a broad and triumphant smile*)
MAVIS (*eagerly*) What was it all about?
BELLAMY (*very pleased with himself*) If I told you, you wouldn't believe me.
MAVIS. Why not?
BELLAMY. Never you mind! By the way, hadn't you got something serious to say to me just before the phone went?
MAVIS. Yes. I—I—(*with a rush*) I just can't marry Dick after all. Now I've seen his home and the sort of life he expects. I know I could never fit in and make him happy. And I'm going to tell him so as soon as possible.
BELLAMY. Hm! And how will *he* take it?
MAVIS. Quite well, I think. I've a hunch he feels the same.
BELLAMY. I see. So you don't want me to go ahead with the divorce?
MAVIS. No.
BELLAMY. Then where does that leave us?
MAVIS (*in a small voice*) Still married, I suppose.

BELLAMY. Well . . . (*After a pause, looking enquiringly at her*) A-ahem!—a reconciliation is always a good stage scene.

MAVIS. But I've already mucked up your new life—and you were so happy.

BELLAMY (*feeling in his pocket and bringing out a newspaper cutting*) There are always openings for a really good butler. (*Giving her the paper*) This, for instance.

MAVIS (*reading*) "Butler and parlour-maid required. (*Glancing briefly at him*) Married couple preferred." (*Looking at him in surprise*) Married couple?

BELLAMY. Exactly.

MAVIS. *Could* we?

(BELLAMY *nods*)

(*She reads again*) "Good wages, liberal table, five in staff . . ."

BELLAMY. Only a small cast, I admit.

MAVIS (*suddenly flinging her arms around his neck; delightedly*) Oh, Trevor, darling! Yes! It's the answer! And it'll be such fun! Oh, what a stupid fool I've been. Can you ever forgive me? (*Breaking off*) Oh dear, that's one of the oldest stage lines ever written.

BELLAMY. Never mind. You're learning. (*Kissing her*) Now this only needs someone to come in and . . .

(LADY WAREHAM *comes in through the double doors*. BELLAMY *and* MAVIS *break apart*)

MAVIS (*quickly*) You just can't go wrong.

LADY WAREHAM. Oh, here you are, Bellamy. Isn't it time for sherry?

BELLAMY. I was just about to bring it, m'lady.

(BELLAMY *goes out* LC.

SIR GEORGE *and* MORTIMER *enter down* L. SIR GEORGE *is carrying his attaché-case and some loose papers*)

SIR GEORGE. Oh, hello, Caroline. Glad you're here. Something important to tell you. (*He starts across the room, sees Mavis and pulls up*)

MAVIS. It's all right, Sir George. I'm just going. I've something important to tell Dick.

(MAVIS *goes out* RC)

SIR GEORGE. Ah! Good, good! (*He dumps the case on the table and turns to Lady Wareham rubbing his hands*) You'll be delighted to know that Mortimer's solved all our problems for us.

MORTIMER. I was only too pleased to advise.

SIR GEORGE (*to Lady Wareham*) I'm going to sell all my War Loan.

LADY WAREHAM. But, George, don't they pay a lot of interest?

SIR GEORGE. Not enough—and always the same. And the damn things themselves never go up. (*Proudly*) I'm going to put the money in a gold mine instead. (*Slapping the papers, prospectuses, etc., down on the table*) See?

LADY WAREHAM (*vaguely glancing at one*) A gold mine? (*After-*

thought) Where they mine gold? (*She looks towards Mortimer for confirmation*)

MORTIMER. Y-yes. That's quite a good description. A little company owns it—Sunbeam Mines Limited. The general belief is that the whole thing is played out. The ten shilling shares stand at only two today.

LADY WAREHAM (*quite misunderstanding*) How terrible!

SIR GEORGE. Not a bit of it. Mortimer has some reliable inside information. They're starting mining again—struck oil, see?

LADY WAREHAM. But why should they strike oil in a gold mine?

SIR GEORGE. Tch! You know what I mean. The shares will go rocketing up. Then I sell out and make an enormous profit.

MORTIMER (*to Lady Wareham*) And *then*, don't you see, he can buy back his War Loan and have several thousands in hard cash left over as well.

LADY WAREHAM. But how wonderful! Let me see, we want a new dining-room carpet and then we can buy . . .

SIR GEORGE (*interrupting*) What a smart fellow you are Mortimer. No wonder you make money.

MORTIMER (*after a sharp look to see if he means anything*) It's just an ordinary business instinct.

SIR GEORGE. Nonsense! It's genius. (*Laughing*) Just to look at you no-one would suspect what you really are.

(MORTIMER *is temporarily taken aback by this and* SIR GEORGE *goes to the table and sits in the chair* R)

Got those transfer forms for me to sign?

MORTIMER (*recovering; taking two forms, one blue, one white, from his pocket*) Here they are! One to buy and one for the War Loan sale. Then off they go to my broker today. We can't risk any delay; the shares may start going up any moment.

SIR GEORGE (*taking out his fountain-pen*) Now, Caroline! Come and witness my signature. Mortimer says he'd rather not because he's so closely associated.

MORTIMER. Wait a bit, Sir George! As your wife, she's not allowed to witness . . .

(BELLAMY *comes in* LC *carrying a tray with a decanter of sherry and glasses*)

Ah, there's Bellamy. He can do it.

SIR GEORGE. Fine. Here, Bellamy, I want you.

BELLAMY. Very good, Sir George. (*He is putting the tray down on the table when he sees the prospectuses, picks one quickly up and glances at it*)

SIR GEORGE (*starting to sign*) Come along. Never mind that. Nothing to do with you.

BELLAMY. No, Sir George. (*He coughs*) Except that the name Sunbeam Mines caught my eye. If you are contemplating a purchase I wonder if I might advise . . .

MORTIMER (*interrupting*) Of course not.

SIR GEORGE. No, of course not.

LADY WAREHAM. Wait, George. Bellamy's advice is always valuable, I'm sure.

SIR GEORGE. But how should he know anything about Sunbeam Mines? How *do* you, Bellamy?

(*During the following dialogue* PAMELA *and* HECTOR *appear on the terrace from the garden and come in through the windows. They are chatting but stop instantly as they realize that something serious is going on, and stay just inside the windows, listening. The others, intent on what* BELLAMY *is saying, do not pay any attention to them*)

BELLAMY (*after a look at Mortimer; turning to Sir George*) By a strange coincidence, sir, one of my erstwhile employers, Sir Willoughby Cripps, was so ill-advised as to invest in that concern. It was explained to him that the shares were extremely low, but this informant had inside knowledge that a rich seam had just been discovered. If he bought them at once he would make a packet—I mean, accumulate a considerable profit.

SIR GEORGE (*with a doubtful look at Mortimer*) But how extraordinary.

LADY WAREHAM. And did he accumulate this packet?

BELLAMY. No, m'lady. Unfortunately, the discovery was not confirmed after all.

SIR GEORGE (*cutting in as Mortimer starts to speak*) You mean he lost his money?

BELLAMY. Indubitably, Sir George.

SIR GEORGE (*turning to Mortimer*) What's all this mean?

MORTIMER (*harassed*) I haven't an idea. May be some wild cat concern with a similar name.

BELLAMY. Perhaps I should add that, even though Sir Willoughby paid what he was told was a very low price, the shares proved to be utterly worthless.

(HECTOR *with* PAMELA *just behind stand listening, puzzled*)

MORTIMER. Need we go into all this nonsense, Sir George? Surely you . . .

SIR GEORGE (*waving him down and speaking to Bellamy*) Who got the money then?

BELLAMY. His friend, sir—a gentleman who it transpired was the actual owner of the shares in Sunbeam Mines and who bought them back later for a song, ready to sell to the next mug—ahem! I mean . . .

(HECTOR *steps quickly forward*)

SIR GEORGE (*cutting in and looking at Mortimer*) What was this fella's name, Bellamy?

(MORTIMER *drops his eyes*)

BELLAMY (*blandly; with a look at Mortimer*) I fear I have entirely forgotten, Sir George.

HECTOR (*looking at Mortimer*) I reckon *I* could make a guess. (*To

Pamela) I said I'd met him some place before, didn't I? I've remembered now. He worked a racket over worthless shares in that same mine over home in Florence a few years ago and got away with twenty thousand dollars from a leading citizen.

LADY WAREHAM. Good gracious!

HECTOR (*looking at Pamela*) And he had first got this citizen's confidence by making love to his daughter and establishing himself as a friend of the family.

PAMELA. Oh! (*She turns away*)

SIR GEORGE (*angry*) Anything to say, Mortimer?

MORTIMER (*in command of himself again*) I don't think so, Sir George. Except that, as the business you invited me to come down and discuss doesn't seem to have materialized, there's really nothing to keep me any longer, is there?

(SIR GEORGE *is about to burst out, but* PAMELA *lays a restraining hand on his arm*)

PAMELA (*coldly; to Mortimer*) No, Mortimer, I don't think there's anything at all.

(MORTIMER *bows slightly and turns to go*)

SIR GEORGE (*angry*) Yes, there is by . . .

PAMELA (*again restraining him*) Father, take mother out on to the terrace and wait till I bring you some sherry—there's a dear.

SIR GEORGE. I . . . I . . . All *right!* (*He turns towards the french windows*)

(LADY WAREHAM *follows him*)

LADY WAREHAM (*as she goes; to Sir George*) I'm glad everything's been explained. It's all *quite* clear now. I suppose this Florence was the citizen's daughter.

(SIR GEORGE *and* LADY WAREHAM *go out at* RC, *turning down* R *and out of sight*)

MORTIMER (*at the double doors*) Well, good-bye.

PAMELA (*coldly*) Good-bye. Bellamy will ring for a taxi for you.

BELLAMY. With the greatest of pleasure, miss. (*He crosses to the phone and dials*)

MORTIMER (*cheerfully*) 'Bye.

(MORTIMER *goes out through the double doors*)

PAMELA. What a beastly thing to happen! Mortimer actually doing that to us! Poor old father would have been caught but for you.

HECTOR. But for Bellamy *I'd* say. What beats me is how . . . (*Turning to Bellamy*) Say, Bellamy, how on earth did you get wise to all this?

BELLAMY. Excuse me, sir. (*Into the receiver*) Will you send a cab to Barwell Towers, please? Yes, at once. To catch the one-ten London train . . . Thank you. (*He replaces the receiver and moves* C) How did I

—er—"get wise", sir? Oh, it was inevitable. It simply *had* to be—by all the rules. There is always a villain in every piece and if he doesn't show in his true colours at first sight, he has to be (*with relish*) unmasked.

HECTOR. Look here! You haven't explained how you *knew*. Of course I said nothing because it was only suspicion, but I cabled my father, and haven't yet had a reply.

BELLAMY. No, sir, but I have.

HECTOR. You?

BELLAMY. Your father rang up here and for some inexplicable reason took me for Sir George.

HECTOR. Well, I'll be . . .

BELLAMY. Quite, sir. But if you will excuse me, I'll see if the—er—departing guest needs help with his luggage.

PAMELA (*awkwardly*) I'm afraid Bellamy is inclined to take a hand in other people's affairs.

HECTOR. Suits me. (*Cheerfully*) He's certainly helped in this one.

PAMELA. What on earth do you mean?

HECTOR. Well, I come over here and discover you. Then I find this Mortimer guy has a kind of option on you, and yet I feel he's not your type and . . . (*He stops*)

PAMELA (*softly*) And what?

HECTOR (*in a rush*) That maybe I *am*.

PAMELA. Oh!

HECTOR. But it's good old Bellamy who swings it for me. Yes, *sir*, *I'll* say I'm all for English butlers.

PAMELA (*pertly*) I think he's been *most* interfering.

HECTOR (*going to her and taking her hand*) Do you?

(*Before she can reply,* SIR GEORGE *re-enters through the french windows followed by* LADY WAREHAM)

SIR GEORGE (*to Pamela*) Where's that damned sherry?

PAMELA. Sorry, Father, I was detained.

LADY WAREHAM. So I perceive. (*To Hector*) Perhaps, Mr Robson, you will be good enough to release my daughter's hand.

PAMELA } (*together*) Why?
HECTOR

(BELLAMY *re-enters* LC *and stands just inside the doors listening*)

LADY WAREHAM. Apparently you have become attached to Pamela, Mr Robson, but as her parents we have to consider your financial and social status.

SIR GEORGE. Financially, particularly, now that Mortimer . . .

LADY WAREHAM. Be quiet, George! (*To Hector*) I have to admit to you, Mr Robson, that we're not wealthy. Therefore any possible suitor for Pamela's hand must be able to support her.

SIR GEORGE. And even *help us* out.

(LADY WAREHAM *rounds on him, and* HECTOR *is about to speak. But before he can do so,* BELLAMY *steps forward*)

BELLAMY. Excuse me, m'lady! If I might mention a small matter?
SIR GEORGE. Why?
LADY WAREHAM. Why not? I keep telling you how helpful Bellamy can be.
BELLAMY. It is simply this, Mr Robson's father at any rate can afford telephone calls from America, and . . .
LADY WAREHAM. From America? (*To Hector*) But your father, Mr Robson, is one of the working classes, I think you said.
HECTOR (*grinning*) Well, *you* said it actually. And he certainly started that way. Just at the moment though he's a building contractor—about the biggest in South Carolina. In fact, he's a millionaire—if it interests you.

(PAMELA *reacts to this*)

SIR GEORGE. Of course it interests me!
LADY WAREHAM. Be quiet, George. (*Beaming effusively at Hector*) But, *Hector*—why didn't you *tell* us?
HECTOR. I guess I . . .
BELLAMY (*interrupting*) I think I can explain that, m'lady. He wished Miss Pamela to love him for himself alone. Shall I take the sherry on to the terrace, m'lady?
LADY WAREHAM. Yes, yes. (*With a look at Hector and Pamela, who are still holding hands*) George!

(BELLAMY *takes the sherry out* RC *and down* R *on to the terrace*)

SIR GEORGE (*seeing Pamela and Hector*) Oh! Oh, yes!

(SIR GEORGE *and* LADY WAREHAM *follow Bellamy out through the french windows and out of sight*)

HECTOR. Well?
PAMELA. Well?
HECTOR. I guess your mother's given me the green light at last.
PAMELA (*mischievously*) Oh? What are you going to do about it?
HECTOR. Marry you—in due course. Meanwhile . . . (*He takes her into his arms*)

(BELLAMY *returns by the french windows*)

BELLAMY. I beg pardon, sir. I'm afraid I timed that entrance rather badly.
HECTOR. To hell with that. You can be the first to congratulate us. We've just gotten engaged.
PAMELA. Aren't you surprised, Bellamy?
BELLAMY (*smoothly*) Not at all, miss. I was convinced from the start that it would work out like this.
PAMELA. Why?
HECTOR. How?
BELLAMY. It always *does* in the third—in the end. My heartiest felicitations.
HECTOR (*looking at him; awed*) Y'know I *still* can't believe in him.

Come to think of it I can't believe anything that's happened to me since I raised my gun to get a rat by the ...

PAMELA. And got me.

HECTOR. And got *you* for keeps.

(*Unseen,* SIR GEORGE *and* LADY WAREHAM *enter through the french windows*)

BELLAMY. If I may be permitted the quip, sir, I should call it *Love at First Shot.*

(*They both laugh*)

(*Very pleased with himself, he raises an imaginary gun and speaks in Sir George's voice*) Girl over! Bang, bang! Got her! My girl, I think, Lord Tyson!

(*They all three laugh delightedly but break off when they notice that Sir George and Lady Wareham have entered and overheard. There is a pause, and then* LADY WAREHAM *breaks suddenly into uncontrolled laughter*)

LADY WAREHAM. Oh dear, oh dear! I never thought I'd do anything but scream if I heard that again, but—oh, Bellamy, it's a wonderful imitation.

SIR GEORGE (*still puzzled*) Imitation? Imitation of what? (*He stares all round until it suddenly dawns*) Gad! It was *me! Me!* (*He starts to laugh*) Me to the life! (*He laughs louder*) Devilish good! By jove, Bellamy, *you* ought to be on the stage!

(*With perfect composure* BELLAMY *moves to the double doors, opens them and turns*)

BELLAMY. I did once consider it, sir, but decided that the life was too unreal.

He goes out with great dignity as—

the CURTAIN *falls*

FURNITURE AND PROPERTY PLOT

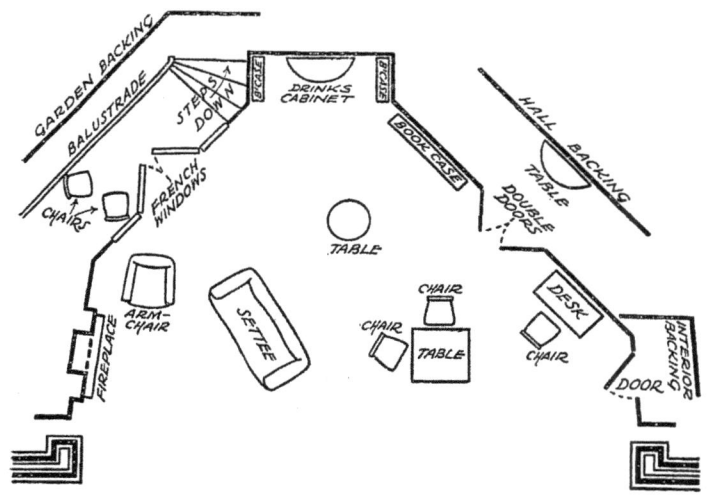

ACT I

On stage: 2 upright chairs
Desk. *On it:* telephone, telephone directories
Desk chair
Oak table. *On it:* magazines, silver cigarette box (full)
    table lighter
Large settee
Armchair
Garden chairs
Drinks cabinet
2 small tables
Who's Who in bookcase L of the alcove
Portraits
Sporting trophies
Native weapons
Ornaments on mantelpiece
Curtains at windows
Cushions for settee and armchair

Off stage: A pipe, newspaper (SIR GEORGE)
Bowl of withered dahlias, first-aid box (LADY WAREHAM)
Silver tray. *On it:* tea for two (BELLAMY)
Cakestand (PRITCHETT)
Suitcase (MAVIS)

Personal: SIR GEORGE: watch, wallet. *In it:* 3 letters, stamp paper
PAMELA: bloodstained handkerchief on L arm
HECTOR: notebook and pencil
MAVIS: handbag

ACT II

Setting as in Act I

Set: Sewing with cotton on settee

Off stage: Empty basket (DICK)
Breakfast cup and saucer (LADY WAREHAM)
2 suitcases, coat, papers (SEATON)
Attaché-case. *In it:* papers (SIR GEORGE)
Basket of mushrooms, tray. *On it:* coffee, biscuits, handbell, pint tankard (BELLAMY)

Personal: SIR GEORGE: diamond tie-pin
LADY WAREHAM: jewelled bracelet
PAMELA: watch

ACT III

Setting as in Act I

Off stage: Hymnal, attaché-case, loose papers (SIR GEORGE)
Salver. *On it:* Sunday papers (*News of the World* on top, *Sunday Times* underneath), small tissue-wrapped parcel. *In it:* handkerchief. Newspaper cutting, tray. *On it:* decanter of sherry and glasses (BELLAMY)
Stamped addressed envelope (MAVIS)
Shoe and loose heel (DICK)
1 blue form, 1 white form (MORTIMER)

Personal: SIR GEORGE: fountain-pen

LIGHTING PLOT

Property fittings required: none
    Interior. The same scene throughout
    THE MAIN ACTING AREAS are RC, C, up C, and LC
    THE APPARENT SOURCE OF LIGHT are french windows RC

ACT I. A September afternoon
To open: Effect of sunlight
No cues

ACT II. A September morning
To open: Effect of sunlight
No cues

ACT III. A September morning
To open: Effect of sunlight
No cues

EFFECTS PLOT

ACT I

Cue 1	At rise of the CURTAIN . *Telephone rings*	(Page	1)
Cue 2	LADY WAREHAM: ". . . be thrown away." *Telephone rings*	(Page	4)

ACT II

Cue 3	PAMELA: ". . . sent to look for him." *Door bang*	(Page	33)
Cue 4	MORTIMER examines papers in case *Jingle of cups off* LC	(Page	46)
Cue 5	MAVIS: ". . . your blasted stage." *Telephone rings*	(Page	49)

ACT III

Cue 6	At the rise of the CURTAIN *Sound of distant church bells*	(Page	51)
Cue 7	MAVIS: "It's like this . . ." *Telephone rings*	(Page	63)

www.ingramcontent.com/pod-product-compliance
Ingram Content Group UK Ltd.
Pitfield, Milton Keynes, MK11 3LW, UK
UKHW021840210426
5322IPUK00022B/389